YOUR PERSONAL LEADERSHIP GUIDE

50 SIMPLE STEPS TO SUCCESS

NTANGEKI NSHALA

REVIEWS

It has been my first time to read an inspirational manuscript of a book authored by a professional banker, and definitely an upcoming business consultant. He has been candid and humble in his attempt to identify from his 15 years experience the factors, attributes and qualities that have contributed to his success.

The intention is to motivate and inspire others to lead themselves better – realize that the abilities and power to succeed are things they have already been given to them by nature/ by the creator and they only need to be unleashed by taking the right attitude and actions.

The author, in my view, correctly spells out fifty (50) personal leadership behaviours, actions and values that need to be observed and nurtured by those aspiring to succeed in their lives. I can assure readers that the qualities and habits he has listed and expounded are in line with those propounded by many other gurus in this subject – indeed he has backed each aspect by citations from other leading writers.

Thus, this book will help many-especially young aspirants – to get basics of success from one source. The book is easy to read and examples given reflect a new generational Tanzanian mind set.

Let me mention a few of the personal leadership behaviours that he has mentioned which I think are critically important: having a vision and setting personal SMART goals and targets, willingness and courage to take action, taking failure as challenge, accepting to do the impossible, determination and commitment, seeking to go an extra mile – to achieve excellence, self development – mentally and physically, and caring for others (the society). These are, but a few of many qualities mentioned in the book.

Once again I wish to reiterate that the book is inspirational and worth reading! I congratulate Mr. Nshala for putting these thoughts together. It is a good starting point for any other writers interested in this subject and people empowerment to add more flesh and personal experiences for the benefit of the general public. I applaud the simplicity of the language used!

Regards

Dr. Charles Kimei
CEO CRDB Bank

Winner of "East African Banker Lifetime Achievement" Award
Banker Africa - East Africa Awards 2016

A transformational guide with valuable and inspiring lessons for emerging leaders.
Jacqueline Woiso
CEO Designate Bank M (Tanzania) Ltd

A spectacular book that will teach you how to take control with a positive attitude that allows you to set goals and priorities, overcome worries, develop self-discipline and pave way for profound, personal happiness…
Neema Kiure Mssusa
Partner Ernest & Young

The author has charted out a broad spectrum avenue to success. If there is an aspect of this avenue to success which the book has not covered, do not bother to know it.
Charles R. B. Rwechungura
Managing Partner CRB Africa Legal & Past President
Tanganyika Law Society

Everyone yearns to be happy and successful in life. Ntangeki Nshala explains very well how to lead yourself to a successful happy life. Read this book and discover how important is personal leadership. I wish you all a fruitful reading of this book for your own success.
Monsignor Deogratias Mbiku *PhD*.
University of Dar es Salaam Catholic Parish.

Many developing countries are aspiring to move to middle income economies in today's globalized world of competition. Leadership skills, application of science and technology are major factors to achieving the goal.

"Your Personal Leadership Guide" is not only a must read book but a also a useful reference for managers, entrepreneurs, leaders of institutions and agents of change.

I applaud the Author Mr. Ntangeki Nshala for his courage to collect his experience and share the tips for self empowerment and success expressed in a simple clear language. This book will be valuable for students of all discipline of life.

Dr. Gertrude Mongella
Former President- Pan African Parliament

YOUR PERSONAL LEADERSHIP GUIDE

50 SIMPLE STEPS TO SUCCESS

NTANGEKI NSHALA

BONABANA

Published by Bonabana Company Limited
Mazinde/Ruvu Street, Plot no. 129, Block A
P. O. Box 79430, Dar es Salaam, Tanzania.
Email: books@bonabana.com
www.bonabana.com

Designed by Zahid Ehsaan

Printed by Bonabana Limited

DEDICATION

In loving memory of my Grandmother
Aurelia Teyelekelerwa Kajumulo, for her
support during my early education.

NTANGEKI NSHALA

If your actions inspire others to dream more, learn more,
do more and become more, you are a leader.

- John Quincy Adams -

TABLE OF CONTENTS

1	Cast your Vision	1
2	Set Smart Goals	6
3	Be Committed and Passionate	10
4	Communicate Effectively	14
5	Attitude	19
6	God's Guidance	24
7	Be Confident	27
8	Manage Your Time	32
9	Stay Focused	36
10	Be Flexible	40
11	Be Creative	43
12	Develop yourself	47
13	Delegate Duties	51
14	Have Integrity	55
15	Share A Smile	58
16	Be Responsible	62
17	Build Character	66
18	Honesty	70
19	Learn To Listen	73
20	Look The Part	77
21	Empower Others	80
22	Learn The Art Of Networking	85
23	Community Service	89
24	Hone Your Public Speaking Skills	92
25	Surround Yourself With Right Friends	96

26   Take Time Off 99
27   Enjoy Leadership Roles 103
28   Be Courageous 106
29   Gain Emotional Intelligence 110
30   Act With Fairness 114
31   Humility 117
32   Embrace Team Spirit 121
33   Eat Well, Live Well 124
34   Embrace Excellence 128
35   Set Meditation Time 133
36   Learn Public Manners 136
37   Practice Empathy 139
38   Persevere Through Challenges 142
39   Walk The Talk 145
40   Have Fun At Work 148
41   Kick Away Bad Habits 151
42   Wake Up Early & Work Hard 155
43   Self-Discipline 159
44   Get A Success Coach 163
45   Personal Branding 167
46   Financial Discipline 170
47   Utilize Technology 173
48   Work-Family Balance 176
49   Learn To Negotiate 180
50   Super Customer Service 183

FOREWORD

It is a great honour for me to write this foreword of the book, "Your Personal Leadership Guide – Simple Steps to Success" written by Mr. Ntangeki Nshala.

The author of this book is a professional accountant, a seasoned banker and now a successful entrepreneur. He is among the few Tanzanians who had the courage of resigning from a lucrative senior banking position to venture into entrepreneurship. After the decision to cross over to the private sector as an entrepreneur, Mr. Nshala quickly learned of the intricacies of entrepreneurship and so far he is doing well. He has developed himself into a reputable keynote speaker on leadership and is an Executive Trainer and a Philanthropist.

Mr. Nshala as he admits himself in his book has had a curious mind since his childhood. Born in a low-income family as the majority of Tanzanians are, he couldn't help but always dream of a better future for himself, a future that would be opposite to the situation he was in. He realized that for his dreams to come true, he needed to be disciplined and focused. He believes that these two attributes have immensely contributed to making him what he is today. On that realization and equipped with the extensive exposure acquired so far he has decided to share his experience with the whole world through the publication of this book.

It is evident from reading the book that the author did extensive reading and research before embarking on writing the book. He has extensively made reference to some prominent personalities world over on the attributes and norms advanced in the book. The personalities quoted in this book include among the many, Albert Schweitzer on happiness; Ben Carson on hard work, perseverance and having faith in God; Bill Gates on setting proper goals and the importance of technology; Thomas Jefferson on the importance of honesty; Zig Ziglar on the relevance of community service; Muhammad Ali on courage; Ken Blanchard and Rick Pitino on humility; Franklin D. Roosevelt and Henry Ford on competition; John F. Kennedy on health; the great Chinese philosopher Confucius excellence; Michael Jordan on dedication and perseverance; Mahatma Gandhi on leading by example.

The many references and quotes cited in this book is a clear indication of the fact that the author went into great length of ensuring the book is of the required standard and quality and that it is relevant to its readers. Having read the book from the first page to the last, I attest with confidence on the quality and relevance of this book.

This is a book comprising of 50 short chapters, where the author goes straight to the heart of an important human attribute/norm showing the reader how these attributes/norms contribute to one's success or failure.

All human beings would like to succeed in whatever they desire to achieve, but most do not know what to do to achieve the desired success. Issues like the right vision; goals; commitment; ability to communicate; having the right attitude; confidence; time management; staying focused; flexibility and creativity; are among the many attributes dealt with in this book which are necessary for one to succeed in whatever one aspires to achieve.

You are going to love reading this book because you will discover that you can immediately stat applying the life-changing attributes and norms in your day to day lifestyle and through doing that enhance the chances of success in your aspirations.

I strongly urge you to get a copy of this book, read it and change your life for the better.

Ludovick S. L. Utouh

(Rtd) Controller and Auditor General and Executive Director WAJIBU – INSTITUTE OF PUBLIC ACCOUNTABILITY.

PREFACE

Since my early childhood, I have always had a curious mind. Born into and brought up in a low-income family, I could not help but to dream of a better future for myself, a future that was opposite my present. I dreamt of a future defined by mental and financial freedom, with a life of abundance, happiness, and success.

I realized that, for my dreams to come true, I had no option but to be both disciplined and diligent. These two qualities have defined me and have made me who I am today.

It is discipline and diligence that have carried me through my school life, my professional studies, and my fourteen years career as a Financial Controller, Senior Banker and a bank Vice President.

Throughout these years, I worked with local and multinational banks, at very senior levels, and I learned a lot of things that are not taught in school.

I had the opportunity to meet various public personalities, banking gurus, prominent lawyers, famed CEOs from public and private sectors, distinguished consultants, multinational business owners, serial entrepreneurs, to mention but a few. As I continuously interacted with these successful people, I slowly began to connect the dots, as to why they have attained such success. I realized that the habits and qualities they possess are common.

After some research and practice, I figured out that many qualities and habits help successful people to continue succeeding in their businesses, and although some of these qualities seem to be common sense, they are not common practice.

In January 2016, I got the idea to compile some of these qualities into a book, so that I could guide those who want to how to lead themselves to success, those who have dreamt of a better future than their childhood and are always searching for guidance.

As Jim Rohn said, "Formal education will make you a living; self-education will make you a fortune." I believe that success is a personal choice, and pursuing that choice will demand a lot of individual effort. It will also require you to hone your talents and align them to accomplish your goals.

It is my hope that this book will add value to your pursuit for success and will shed light on your path towards realizing your dream.

I will also be happy to receive your feedback so that my next book can be better and address a topic that is relevant to many.

Ntangeki Nshala

ntangeki@ntangekinshala.com

ACKNOWLEDGEMENT

I would like to express my gratitude to people who saw me through this book; Babuu Joseph, Lydia Nyachuro, Charity Mwakyoo, Lara Ramsay and Amelia Coward for reading, editing and offering useful thoughts that have made this book possible.

Thanks to my children, Ishengoma, Nyakato and Kiiza for bringing joy to my life and being a reason for me to keep moving.

Above all special thanks to the love of my life, my wife, Theodosia for her continued encouragement and support and for always filling my heart with love and peace.

INTRODUCTION

What is success? What makes a person successful? Why are so many people not successful? How is success recognized and measured?

These are probably some of the questions that have been flowing through your mind. The same questions used to flow through mine before I decided to research this vast subject and make observations that allowed me to understand success and all of its attributes better.

Throughout my fifteen year career as an accountant and a banker, I worked with various banks, local and multinational, and I got the opportunity to meet many people who were very successful in their endeavors: business owners, consultants, entrepreneurs and CEOs of public and private corporations.

In our daily lives, we hear of people who have done well in their fields; Business gurus like Bill Gates, Richard Branson and Aliko Dangote. Sports stars like: Floyd Mayweather, Mbwana Samatta, and Christiano Ronaldo. Musicians like Michael Jackson, Beyonce Knowles and Diamond Platnumz. Success is possible in every field and comes in many forms.

Being successful is simple, but not easy. All the successful people I know have discovered the secret and have made deliberate efforts to acquire the habits that lead to success.

In that regard, success is a choice. To be precise, success is a personal choice. No one can choose to be successful for you. You have to make that decision, and you will have to go down the path yourself.

While you go down that road, you will need guidance, and that is why I have written this book, Your Personal Leadership Guide. This book will help you to know what it takes to be successful. This book will help you to realize that the source of success is more of a mental status than money.

If you want to be successful in your life, this is the book for you. It will give you important qualities that you need to acquire to change your behavior so that you become successful.

This book will show you that success is simple to achieve but not easy. In that regard, you will have to write down your vision, dreams and goals then plan how to pursue them.

A famous adage says, "if you do not know where you are going, any road can take you there." This is exactly what happens to many people who spend their time wishing for a better life, but have not taken any steps to know how they change it. Year after year, they keep doing the same things, the same way, which gives them the same results.

If you want an extraordinary life, you have to be ready to do extraordinary things. If you want to be the best in your field, you have to learn and deliver better services than any other, and that means you will have to work harder than all of your competitors.

These ideas and many others have been compiled in this book, and that is why I call it, Your Personal Leadership Guide. Its sole purpose is to help you lead yourself into success. To help you be the best you can be, and eventually, become what God created you to be.

1

CAST YOUR VISION

The only thing worse than being blind is having sight but no vision.
- Helen Keller -

As a child, I was terrified of the dark so much so that if the lights went off I would instantly start to cry out for help. In the darkness, I had illusions of a monster-like figure and as a child, I assumed they were about to eat me alive. I never felt safe. To this day I hate darkness. Walking along a path without a clear vision makes me uncomfortable because I love to be in control of my journey. But come to think of it, in our world, many people in their daily lives walk in darkness.

The darkness I refer to in this situation is the lack of a clear vision for one's life. What one wants to achieve in their life. What talents they have and how to develop them so as to serve humanity. This is because talents are not meant only to benefit the bearer but are specifically planted in each person to serve the world. When talents are utilized as prescribed by God, they make the holder happy and the world a better place. Talents are like gemstone buried deep in the soul and can only be mined when there is a need. Mining as you know, takes time and determination, first for exploration and then digging to find the minerals. When found, minerals are in a rough state and thus need polishing before we can see their real value. No one spends time and money mining for a gemstone if they do not know its perceived value. One needs first to determine the value that the gemstone will bring to them. This clarity required of miners is the type of vision that everyone needs to have in their lives. Many people live out their days not doing much or doing something that does not make them satisfied or happy.

Every person entered this world to fill a spot in a huge puzzle that God created. You have a spot too, and it can never be occupied by any other person, as they will not fit. Every spot in a puzzle has a unique shape; only one person can mold himself or herself into the form of that spot. That person is you. Dr. Myles Munroe said, "I think the greatest gift God ever gave a man is not the gift of sight but the gift of vision. Sight is the function of the eyes, but vision is the function of the heart."

To be successful in your life, you need to have a clear vision of what it is exactly you want to be or what it is that you want to accomplish. Your life vision has to be clear and precise. Any lack of clarity in your vision will cause missteps and wastage of time as you try to accomplish it.

People become successful in their lives because they have sought clarity for their vision. They know what they want, and they follow their dreams. A person with vague aspirations will end up with vague results and will always be unhappy with his life.

Last week I was speaking at a Rotary fellowship meeting, and someone commented that vision is important for leaders but not for every person. My response was that all people are born leaders. What differentiates them is that some mine and polish their leadership talents and skills and others keep them buried.

In that case, everyone is a leader, and the least number of followers a leader can have is one, and that one is you. You can lead yourself to glory or destruction, happiness or sadness. You might ask yourself, how do you get to understand your true vision and whether this vision will go beyond just making yourself happy? Will it allow you to earn a living enough to run your life and settle all your monthly bills? I can assure you that success does not make you happy but rather happiness is what will bring you success.

When you find your spot in life, you will change your view of what you are doing from a job to a hobby. Your mind and energy will be so focused on it that you will have days when you forget to eat. This way, you will become brilliant at what you do, and your products will be unmatched in the market.

You will polish all talents that accompany that hobby and soon, you will start making more than you ever thought you would and you will be having fun too.

Your vision and actions have to be well aligned. Vision without action is a mere dream and action without vision is wastage of resources, but when vision is well aligned with action great things can be accomplished. It is not by accident that some people become successful in what they do, be they musicians like Michael Jackson, artists like Michelangelo, soccer stars like Christiano Ronaldo, politicians like Barack Obama or religious leaders like Pope Francis. It is what they are born to do.

If you can tune into your purpose, really align with it, and set goals so that your vision is an expression of that purpose, then life will flow much more smoothly. Hellen Keller once said that the only thing worse than being blind is having sight but no vision. Developing a vision will require you to dig deep into your soul and find your life's purpose. This process requires time. You need set aside time for meditation.

Think through, what it is that you love doing that makes you feel happy and satisfied. What is it that you are eager to do for hours, that you are even ready to skip your lunch to have it accomplished? What is it that does not feel like work to do, even though it requires your energy and imagination? When you are at it remember what Cecil Beaton said, "Be daring, be different, be impractical, be anything that will assert integrity of purpose, and imaginative vision against the play-it-safers, the creatures of the commonplace, the slaves of the ordinary."

Make your vision big! Nelson Mandela said that "there is no passion for being found playing small - in settling for a life that is less than the one you are capable of living. Do not worry if your dream seems to be too big to be accomplished, because all significant developments in the history of humanity are a result of brave people, those who pursued dreams that were thought to be impossible. Your vision has to be extraordinary.

The process of developing your vision will act as a request to yourself to bring out the best lying within you. It is a demand to unlock your brilliance that will turn you into an expert in your area, make you live a purposeful life and create a legacy for generations. Your vision statement should be a statement which echoes your life purpose, goals, and intentions.

"The first step toward creating an improved future is developing the ability to envision it. Vision will ignite the fire of passion that fuels our commitment to do whatever it takes to achieve excellence. Vision has no boundaries and knows no limits. Our vision is what we become in life." - Tony Dungy

It is a fact of life that if you do not have an ultimate goal, your life will be defined by a lack of direction, a lack of accomplishment, and a lack of meaning. If you do not know where you are going, any road will take you there.

All successful people are aware of that, which is why they are big dreamers. They imagine what their future could be, in every respect, and they work every day towards that distant vision. As stated by Jack Welch, *"Good business leaders create a vision, articulate the vision, passionately own the vision, and relentlessly drive it to completion."*

You, also, must develop your life vision and implement it so that when you stand at the end of your life and look back, you can proudly say with absolute confidence that, "I lived my life in such a way that I was true to the very essence of who I was meant to be."

2

SET SMART GOALS

The vision must be followed by the venture. It is not enough to stare up the steps - we must step up the stairs. **- Vance Havner -**

Vision is knowing how high you want to climb to reach the peak of your happiness and success. Vision is many times referred as a dream. Many motivational speakers already tell us to dream big because it takes the same amount of energy and time to dream small. So no matter what dream BIG!! Bill Gates says that *"if your dream does not scare you, maybe it is not big enough."*

But to climb to that level of success, you will need a ladder or stairs. These stairs will enable you to move step by step towards your **vision.** These stairs are what we call goals joined to form the whole staircase which is a strategic plan.

If you want to progress towards your personal vision and dreams, you will need to take daily intentional steps. You will be required to set realistic short-term and long-term goals aligned with your vision. Focusing on your goals allows you to move forward in the direction of your vision.

You might wonder what exactly are goals and how are they **different from the vision.** One of America's finest motivator, Earl Nightingale, summarized it by saying, "We are at our very best, and we are happiest when we are fully engaged in the work we enjoy on the journey toward the goal we've established for ourselves. It gives meaning to our time off and comfort to our sleep. It makes everything else in life so wonderful, so worthwhile."

In that regard, after developing a clear vision of who you want to be or what you want to accomplish, you must devise a step by step plan to move towards realizing the grand vision. Setting goals is a process that will also require you to think deeply about the sequence of steps to be made and resources to be mobilized.

Your goals have to be motivating but challenging. They have to be goals that induce a sense of urgency in you. Goals that will need you to start now, but at the same time, will need you to stretch your capabilities. They should require more work, time and attention.

You will have to write down the goal and explain to yourself why that goal is valuable. The larger the why, the more the reason to push through towards your goal. Some people like to show it to their friends and explain to them why they want to follow that particular goal. This process of explaining your goal to others gives you a chance to make the goal clearer to you. Your friends do not necessarily have to approve of it because they might find the goal too big to comprehend and subsequently discourage you. There is a theory in goal setting that many people use which you can also apply called SMART, which refers to; Specific, Measurable, Attainable, Relevant, and Time-bound.

Specific means your goal must be clear and well defined. A blurred goal is unhelpful because it does not help to guide you. A well-defined goal will shorten your journey towards achieving your vision. For example, "I will reduce my fuel expenses by 10 percent this year," if fuel is one of your major expenditures among many expenses that will make sense. So instead of generalizing 'expenses', you make it explicit, fuel expenses.

When a goal is said to be measurable, it means that it includes precise sizes, amounts, dates, and so on that will help you or anyone else measure your degree of success. Without a way to measure your success, you miss out on the happiness and satisfaction that comes with knowing that you have achieved something that will eventually motivate you to move forward. For example, "I will reduce my fuel expenses by 10 percent this year," the 10% gives you something to measure against.

You have to set attainable goals. These are goals that you believe can be reached with full effort and focus. These goals must challenge and scare you. Goals that scares you will force you to reach into your inner power. If Barrack Obama had not set a seemingly unattainable goal, he would not have become President of the United States. If Steve Jobs had not wanted to create an instrument that would revolutionize the tools we use to communicate, he would not have made iPhones, iPads, and iPods.

Your goal has to be relevant in helping you to realize your vision and not otherwise. If you wish to become a neurosurgeon like Ben Carson, and you are in secondary school you will need to pick science subjects pass your high school with good grades and apply for a medical school. Later you will specialize in neurosurgery and work hard to become a top specialist like Ben Carson. A process like this will apply in any profession, be it football, law, or so on.

For your goal to be time bound Napoleon Hill summarized it for you, *"A goal is a dream with a deadline"* Your goal must have a deadline. Again, this means that you know when you can celebrate success. When you are working on a deadline, your sense of urgency increases and achievement will come that much quicker. For example, "I will reduce my fuel expenses by 10 percent this year," The timeline, 'this year', will enable you to evaluate your performance. After you have gone through the SMART process and have solidified your goals, you will have to write them down. Writing them down will help you to remember them well.

My personal practice has been putting them at places that I know will be visible to me almost all of the time. I put my written goals in my bedroom next to my dressing table. When am getting dressed for work, I look at them. When I am in the office, I also look at them because I have placed a list of them on the wall on my right-hand side. You will have to do that too. A constant reminder will help you keep focused on them.

You will also be required to review your goals regularly in order to see how your action plan is progressing. Regular reviews will compel you to revisit the implementation of your action plan and bring you back on track in case you had lost direction. You do not have to wait until the end of the year to know whether you are on track, or you are losing focus.

3

BE COMMITTED AND PASSIONATE

Generally speaking, I think that if you do anything with commitment and passion, it will come good. **- Kevin McCloud -**

You might have your vision very clear and the goals well outlined, but if you have no commitment and passion for accomplishing your goals you will achieve nothing. Your dream will be elusive, and your goals will just lie on the drawing board. Most people know what they want to do in life but just haven't pursued it because they are too attached to their comfort, safety or simplicity of their routines. If you want to achieve your dreams in life, you must be willing to detach yourself from your comfort zone and commit to a new style of life that will result in new wins.

Mario Andretti said, "Desire is the key to motivation, but it's determination and commitment to an unrelenting pursuit of your goal - a commitment to excellence - that will enable you to attain the success you seek."

Please note that, in this world, you will not get what you want but what you are 100% committed. In other words, unless you are fully committed to something, you cannot hope to turn your desires into reality. To commit to something is about passion. The level of passion you can gather from the inside of you will determine the degree of achievement that you will attain in whatever you will do. Passion is what will help you to overcome your doubts during difficult moments along your success journey. "Surprisingly, it is often the little, fixable things that get in our way," Reeder says.

Napoleon Hill, in his classic book, Think and Grow Rich, claims, "The starting point of all achievement is desire. Keep this constantly in mind. Weak desires bring weak results, just as a small amount of fire makes a small amount of heat." The reason for you to pursue your goals has to be clear and vigorous in your soul. You will have to be passionate about your goal and your larger vision. When you have passion, you will produce energy that will help you to move forward towards accomplishing your goal. Donald Trump said, "Without passion, you don't have energy, without energy you have nothing." Therefore passion will induce energy into what you do.

John Wesley has stated, "When you set yourself on fire, people love to come and see you burn." Passion increases influence, and it will attract people and resources towards you because people will want to be a part of what's going on. If you want to increase your influence, then you need to be passionate about what you do. You might remember David Beckham, the Manchester United soccer player. He was so passionate about soccer that he spent most of his day on the training pitch. After displaying his skills during matches, people began to love everything about him, and he became more than a soccer star. Your passion for your dreams and goals will attract new opportunities and open doors of success.

When you are passionate about what you do, it moves you closer to your full potential, helps you to achieve more results, thus moving you to the next level within your career or personal journey.

George Santayana, a 20th-century philosopher, poet, essayist, and novelist, says: "Nothing so much enhances a good as to make sacrifices for it." To achieve your goal and dream, you must be willing to sacrifice. Sacrifices come in many forms depending on your vision and environment, but they will be there. Because, for you to achieve what only a few people have achieved, you must be willing to push yourself to the level that only a few people have managed to push themselves.

If you are an amateur athlete and want to be number one like Usain Bolt you will have to train as hard as Usain Bolt trains and even more. This means foregoing other comforts and leisure, time with friends, family, and even other life opportunities.

If you want to be the best entrepreneur in your industry, you have to outperform your competitors with efficient use of resources, high quality of products and new designs that are not yet in the market. This means long working hours and intense monitoring of results. Sacrifice will mean being ready to focus on your goals and not letting other activities interfere, even if your life will be impacted by missing out on other activities. Nelson Mandela was jailed for 27 years but did not give up his fight for equality in his country and, eventually, he succeeded.

Virat Kohli said, "whatever you want to do, do with full passion and work hard towards it. Don't look anywhere else. There will be a few distractions, but if you can be true to yourself, you will be successful for sure". Distractions will always be present because the road to glory is never smooth. Your determination to stand against all obstacles, to stand up after being knocked down, is what will allow you to achieve your goals. Keep your dreams alive. Understand that achieving anything requires faith and belief in yourself, your vision, hard work, determination, and dedication. Remember, all things are possible for those who believe.

The quality of a person's life is in direct proportion to their commitment to excellence, regardless of their chosen field of endeavor -Vince Lombardi

You must also note that to achieve your goals, and there are always small wins that we keep recording along the way. Since we already set goals that are measurable, these little wins have to be registered, recognized and celebrated. Because, when you celebrate the small wins you become energized and motivated to move forward. These wins will help your mind prepare for the next hurdle, even if it is harder than the earlier one.

4

COMMUNICATE EFFECTIVELY

No matter how much success you're having, you can't continue working together if you can't communicate. **- Matt Cameron -**

Warren Buffet once told a class of business students that better communication could boost their value by fifty percent. Why do you think this business mogul said that? I remember, when I was in secondary school, a communication teacher once gave us a good example of how information is lost when it gets transmitted from one person to another.

I remember he made students stand in a circle and told the first student some words that the first student would tell the second; the second would tell the third and so on till the tenth. By the time the tenth was asked what message he had received it was entirely different from what the teacher had told the first student.

This exercise has stuck with me until today and is a clear example of how bad communication can cause loss of information and result in unintended outcomes.

Communication is the process whereby two parts transfer information between themselves. When the conveyed information, thoughts or intentions are well transferred as intended, then that is good communication, but when some meaning is lost in the process, then that is bad communication.

Tony Robins says, "To effectively communicate, we must realize that we are all different in the way we perceive the world and use this understanding as a guide to our communication with others."

Successful people are good communicators. They have learned that effective communication is about authenticity in how they speak or write. Communication and success are intertwined. It would be difficult to lead and motivate others if you do not communicate in an authentic way.

Your failure to communicate effectively will deter you from achieving your career goals and also has the potential to affect your social and personal relationships. From the above introduction, it has become very clear that wherever you are and whatever your ambitions are, your communication skills are vital to your success. Whether you are an executive in a corporation, a team leader, a salesperson or the Chief Executive Officer of a company, you will need to communicate with your peers, prospective customers or your bosses.

You have to put communication skills down as one of improvement area, and you will have to practice these skills until they become perfect.

Dianna Booher, one of the business communication gurus, digs into communication failures in her book, *What More Can I Say*, and discusses what you can do about them. She gives you examples of messages that succeed along with a practical nine-point checklist that addresses the common reasons why your communication is inhibiting you from achieving your goals. Her goal is to help you build stable relationships, increase your credibility, get your point across clearly, and become a more influential communicator. I do not have to reinvent the wheel; I am only putting them down for you to internalize. You can buy Dianna Booher's book for a detailed explanation.

Generate trust rather than distrust - Effective communication requires trust in you, your message and your delivery. We tend to trust people who are like us, or we have social proof that others trust, or we feel reciprocal trust from the sender. Individuals who are optimistic, confident, and demonstrate competence generate trust. Are you one of these?

Be collaborative rather than present a monolog - Collaborating for influence has become a fundamental leadership skill. Be known for the questions you ask – not the answers you give. Statements imply that you intend to control the interaction, whereas questions imply that another input has value to arriving at a mutually beneficial decision.

Aim to simplify rather than inject complexity - Simplicity leads to focus, which produces clarity of purpose. People distrust what they don't understand, what they perceive as doublespeak, or things made unnecessarily complicated. Influencing people to change their mind or actions requires building a simple, intuitive path to your answer.

Deliver with tact and avoid insensitivity - Some word choices turn people off because they are tasteless, tactless, or pompous. Phrase your communication to avoid biases that might create negative reactions. Consider using other authority figures or quotes to deliver a more persuasive message while eliminating any sensitive implications.

Position future potential instead of achievements alone - The allure of potential is usually greater than today's actual results. This is especially true for career advancement, motivation, and the power of systems. For customers and clients, let them have it both ways. Consider what you can package as your untapped potential.

Consider the listener perspective rather than the presenter - Audiences tend to average all the pieces of information they hear and walk away with a single impression. More is not always better, so reduce the length of presentations and speeches. Perceptions are more important than reality. Avoid the over-helpfulness syndrome.

Tend toward specifics rather than generalizations - Many executive speeches miss the mark because they aim for the general constituency and hit no one. People need to know how a message relates to them personally, not just what has to be done and why. Your challenge is to make the future seem attainable and applicable to each listener.

Capitalize on emotions as well as logic - Emotion often overrides logic, but logic rarely overrides emotion. For many listeners, a logical explanation merely justifies and supports an emotional decision that has already been made.

Recognize and calm first any emotional reactions of fear. Engage multiple senses to reach a listener's emotion.

Lead with empathy before your perspective - Empathy starts with active listening to what is being said and what is not being said. Listen for the gaps and distortion between perception and reality, and then focus on closing these gaps before any persuasion to your own perspective is attempted. Let others help you listen, and tune your response.

You will appreciate that effective communication is essential to your personal success, and all these highlighted areas need practice to become a truly effective communicator.

As Yehuda Berg puts it, "Words are singularly the most powerful force available to humanity. We can choose to use this force constructively with words of encouragement, or destructively using words of despair. Words have energy and power with the ability to help, to heal, to hinder, to hurt, to harm, to humiliate and to humble." In that regard, effective usage of words can propel you toward your dreams.

5

ATTITUDE

Your attitude, not your aptitude, will determine your altitude.
- Zig Ziglar -

Research has shown that success is; 80% Attitude and 20% Aptitude. I cannot agree more! Zig Ziglar worded it, "Your attitude, not your aptitude, will determine your altitude". So where will your success altitude be? At sea level or the top of Mount Kilimanjaro? It is your choice.

This reminds me of the example I heard about two marketing research executives who were sent to a foreign land to search for new markets for shoes. The two officials arrived in that foreign land and toured around. The area was inhabited by people who were economically active, but no one wore shoes. They all walked barefoot.

When the two researchers went back home, they wrote two different reports. The first one reported that the place had no market for shoes because those people do not wear shoes. The second executive reported with a lot of excitement that they had discovered a gold mine, a game changer, a virgin market.

How come the two executives came up with two different reports about the same market? It is all in their attitude.

Your attitude will make you react to things or situations in a particular manner. It will make you see opportunities or just let them pass by you unnoticed. They say every cloud has a silver lining.

Your attitude will make you focus your attention either on the cloud or the silver lining. It is your attitude that will make you see a glass of water half full or half empty.

Your attitude towards something can either be positive or negative. A positive attitude towards a particular thing will ignite within you a chain of positive reactions of positive thoughts, events and outcomes and may help spark extraordinary results. On the other hand, a negative attitude towards a particular thing will trigger a chain of negative reactions that can affect your mood and judgment which will give you poor, undesired results.

Psychologists define attitude as a psychological tendency that is expressed by evaluating things with some degree of favor or disfavor.

A clear vision in your mind can be equated with living in a clean house. You may have a big clear vision for your life, developing a positive attitude is like cleaning your house. Your life will have many components, same as a good house. Since with a dirty house, the good life cannot be achieved, with a prejudiced mind, success cannot be attained.

Cleaning your house is same as removing bad attitudes in your mind. Positive thinking will remove all dirty, bad behaviors and make you understand people around you without judging them. The greatest thing about attitude is that it is the one thing we all have the ability to control. It is a choice. According to Viktor E. Frankl, "our greatest freedom is the freedom to choose our attitude."

You can choose to be hopeful or helpless, dream or doubt. You can choose to see in others strengths or flaws, accepting or judging them. You can live in this world focusing on opportunities or problems and yes you can choose to be embracing or resisting.

A positive attitude or what some refer to as positive thinking is crucial for your personal leadership and success. It will strengthen you while passing through rough patches and it will open doors of opportunities. Brian Tracy tells you, "to develop an attitude of gratitude, and give thanks for everything that happens to you, knowing that every step forward is a step toward achieving something bigger and better than your current situation."

According to Thomas Jefferson, "Nothing can stop the man with the right mental attitude from achieving his goal; nothing on earth can help the man with the wrong mental attitude." If you want to succeed, you have to develop a positive mental attitude.

Ability is what you're capable of doing. Motivation determines what you do. Attitude determines how well you do it -Lou Holtz

Developing positive attitude is simple but not easy, you will need conscious determination and continuous practice until you master it with perfection. I am putting down some tips for you on how to develop a positive attitude but you will have to search more within yourself if you want to succeed in life and live at the top of your potential.

Visualize Success - Vision is the portrayal of your mental picture of the future. People with a positive attitude have a clear vision of the future and a deep belief that they can turn their vision into a reality.

Focus on goals - Successful people set goals and then take the daily actions needed to turn their vision and goals into a reality.

Engage in Positive Self-Talk - You think by using words. These words create emotion and determine our attitude. If you use good encouraging words, you will be happy and energized, but, if you use wrong words, you will create anger and hate in your mind. When you are happy with your life, and you are using kind words to describe to yourself just how blessed you are, bad attitude simply will not appear. Choose your words wisely!

Keep good company - the people that you spend most of your time with will have a significant influence on you; positively or negatively. It is hard to be positive about life when you only hang out with people of a negative demeanor. Your brain can not resist the temptation of accepting thoughts that are frequently presented to it. Select your associates carefully.

Take responsibility - in a study identifying the most common career-limiting habits, the common phrase, "It's Not My Job," came in second place. This is an example of a bad attitude. You cannot expect a promotion in future with this kind of attitude. To a customer, you are the organization, so you must always take the initiative to make a client feel comfortable while trying to reach out to the proper person to serve him.

Maintain a Sense of Humor - Having the ability to think funnily, laugh and not to take yourself too seriously when things go wrong helps in the maintenance of a positive attitude. Learn to laugh often.

Find your spot - When you are in the right spot, you will love what you do, and you will be happy. Happiness will induce a positive attitude which will propel you to success.

Stay mentally fit - When you do what you know you should do and don't do what you know you shouldn't do, you feel better about yourself. When you feel good about yourself, positive thoughts lead to a positive attitude.

Stay focused on results - Every successful person has faced personal or family challenges that have had a significant impact on their attitude. These challenges can cause negative feelings which can influence your attitude and drag you down. Don't let them. Stay focused on achieving positive results at work.

Listen attentively - Successful people listen and observe how their teams are motivated. If morale is flat or down, it may be related to your attitude. Conversely, when the team is up and highly motivated, there is also a good chance that it is related to your attitude. It is important to Listen, observe and determine what attitude you want to project to your team. They say, "A bad attitude is contagious . . . Fortunately, so is a positive attitude. The choice is yours".

6

GOD'S GUIDANCE

Through hard work, perseverance and faith in God,
you can live your dreams. **- Ben Carson -**

We now live in the times when we have many people of various faiths living together working hand in hand. Some do not believe in God at all. I believe in the existence of God, who is the Almighty, the one who blesses us with all that we seek. That is why we pray, we go to church, to the mosque, to synagogues, to all kinds of houses of Worship. All these are efforts to tap into the power of God. Abdul Kalam, former President of India, said, "God, our Creator, has stored within our minds and personalities, great potential strength and ability. Prayer helps us tap into and develop these powers."

This means that with all of the human efforts that we put into achieving what we wish to achieve, there is another supernatural power which has the influence on our ability to realize it.

Iyanla Vanzant said, in my deepest, darkest moments, what got me through was a prayer. Sometimes my prayer was 'Help me.' Sometimes a prayer was 'Thank you.'

What I've discovered is that intimate connection and communication with my Creator will always get me through because I know my support, my help, is just a prayer away.

"Trust in the Lord with all your heart; do not depend on your own understanding." Faith plays an active role in every person's success. It is considered to be a constructive force for good and can have an enormous influence in promoting positive relationships. Faith is what energizes us through the long and tough road towards our personal success.

It does not matter what religion you follow; be it Hindu, Judaism, Islam, Traditional or Christianity. Faith in God gives you the ultimate purpose of living. Faith gives us peace of mind. Faith in God guides you on how you relate to your business partners, colleagues, subordinates, and your friends. Faith in God shapes your attitude which then plays a vital role in your personal success.

Kirk Cameron said, "Faith in God produces character; character will produce courage, courage to face the challenges of the day."

Many people start their working day with players. For most people, the first thing they do when they wake up is praying. Early morning is the best time for prayers because your mind is almost pure, with no distractions. It is the time to thank God for granting you yet another day but also seeking His divine intervention and guidance in whatever you do during the day.

Faith builds and tests discipline. This reminds me of a friend of mine whom I work with. He is a truly devout Muslim and does not miss the prayers every Friday. If it happens that we have a meeting on a Friday, and the agenda is not complete, He will quietly walk out of the room and head to the nearby mosque. He does not miss the prayers, no matter what is on the table.

This is what commitment means. Commitment to God. God comes first. God should come first for you too, in whatever you do. It is a good test of one's character. If you can keep your commitment to God, whom you do not see, it is possible to maintain commitment with partners that you work and rub shoulders with regularly.

7

BE CONFIDENT

When you have confidence, you can have a lot of fun.
And when you have fun, you can do amazing things. **- Joe Namath -**

If you want to be successful in life, you have no option but to be confident in yourself. The definition of self-confidence is a feeling of trust in one's abilities, qualities, and judgment.

The key word here is feeling. It means becoming confident takes just adjusting your feelings about yourself. It is an issue with your mindset. What a simple skill to acquire! But very necessary, for without confidence the vision will remain a dream, the goals will gather dust on the drawing board, all commitments will turn into frustrations, your communication strategy will be shelved, and your faith in God will be tested. Lack of self-confidence comes because you think you are weak, not capable, not on the same level with others. You pull yourself down. You kill yourself.

Marcus Garvey also said, "if you have no confidence in self, you are twice defeated in the race of life but with confidence, you have won before you have started."

Successful people are confident people. Self-confident people are admired by others and inspire confidence in others. Confident people have fears, but they face their fears head-on and tend to be risk takers. They know and trust their capabilities to overcome eventually whatever obstacles that come their way. Self-confident people tend to focus their attention on the positive side of their challenges. They are content with themselves. As Diane Arbus said, "regardless of how you feel inside; always try to look like a winner. Even if you are behind, a sustained look of control and confidence can give you a mental edge that results in victory."

"Low self-confidence isn't a life sentence. Confidence can be learned, practiced, and mastered--just like any other skill. Once you master it, everything in your life will change for the better." --Barrie Davenport

Ten years ago, I could not stand in public and speak a single straight sentence. My brain seemed to stop functioning whenever I stood in public to say something. If I had to, my hand would become sweaty in less than a minute; my heart would miss some beats, and my joints would lose their grip. I felt this way since childhood. But when I had a goal that required me to speak in public, I decided to learn how to overcome this fear. It was simple, and it worked, and the rest is history. If I did it, why can't you?

Even the greatest leaders and successful people lack self-confidence at certain times. Self-confidence is not a static quality; rather, it's a mindset that takes the effort to maintain when the going gets tough.

It must be learned, practiced and mastered just like any other skill. But once you master it, you will be changed for the better. Like Robert Kiyosaki puts it, confidence comes from discipline and training. Since self-confidence can be developed and maintained,

I will share a few tips that will help you gain this important feeling and allow you to move towards accomplishing your goals and live your dream.

Body Language - Your body language can instantly demonstrate self-assuredness, or it can scream failure. Portray yourself in a manner that exudes confidence and radiate mastery and control. When you look confident, you will gain self-assurance and people will have much more confidence in you.

Hold your head high, sit up straight, gently bring your shoulders back to align your spine and look directly at the other person when interacting. Do not offer a floppy handshake and maintain good eye contact while someone is speaking to you.

Smiling will make you feel better, and others feel more comfortable around you. Try to visualize a person with good posture and a smile and you will see a confident person.

Dress Well - When you look good, you feel good. When you select appropriate clothing and accessories for the occasion, you will automatically increase your self-esteem. Dress up for success, or for the next position to which you wish to get promoted. Let your personality shine through your accessories. Bold jewelry or a colorful tie can be a focal point and a good conversation starter.

Style your hair and give yourself a clean shave. Not only will this make you feel better about yourself, but others will be more likely to perceive you as successful and self-confident.

Speak with energy - Listen to professional speakers and observe how they deliver their speeches. All experienced speakers speak confidently, in a steady, rhythmic tone. They use pauses to emphasize ideas.

Speak slowly - Research has proven that those who take the time to speak slowly and clearly feel more self-confidence and appear more self-confident to others. Adopt a firm way of speaking that indicates your confidence. You will feel your self-esteem begin to rise. To be taken seriously, avoid high-pitched, nervous chatter or twittering giggles in your speech. People will listen to you more attentively when they see confidence radiate from within you.

Develop a positive attitude - Low self-confidence is often caused by the negative thoughts running through our minds on an endless track. If you are always criticizing yourself and saying you're not good enough, aren't attractive enough, aren't smart enough or athletic enough, you are creating a self-killing prophecy.

You will eventually become what you are preaching inside your mind, and that is toxic. Smile, laugh, be funny and surround yourself with confident, positive people. You will feel better, and people around you will enjoy your company.

Be an Active Participant - You must be active. Practice makes perfect. Practice being confident by walking to a stranger at a networking event and introducing yourself. Ask questions and look straight into the eyes of the person. Through this, you will be perceived as confident and successful. Action breeds confidence and courage. While attending a business meeting or conference, listen attentively and ask intelligent questions. All participants will note your presence. If you commit more energy to developing your positive traits, your confidence will start to shine through.

Be Organized - a few years ago I was taught in a seminar about the five P's: Prior Planning prevents poor performance. When you are organized and prepared, you become confident. Preparation will help you to plan for unforeseen circumstances in life. It is like predicting future events and preparing how to react to them.

Be an expert in your industry, your subject matter, your goals and what drives you towards success. Before you start a task, first imagine how you want to feel once you have completed it, it will motivate you to complete it no matter what.

8

MANAGE YOUR TIME

My favorite things in life don't cost any money. It's really clear that the most precious resource we all have is time. **- Steve Jobs -**

Time is the most valuable asset every human being has been given. Surprisingly, some people use time and achieve quite a lot while others seem not to realize much. But, since time is so valuable, the ones who master the efficient usage of their time are the ones who will succeed. It is very difficult to find a successful person who spends time uneconomically. There is a popular adage that says, "there is no hurry in Africa."

Samuel Smiles said, "Lost wealth may be replaced by industry, lost knowledge by study, lost health by temperance or medicine, but lost time is gone forever."

If you want to be successful, you have no option but to master the art of time management. People with a vision to realize and goals to accomplish will always be cautious about how they utilize every minute of their day. 24 hours will not be enough in a day.

Time management just means organizing your daily activities, including the amount of time that you will spend on each activity so that no time is wasted not knowing what tasks follow after another. The first method to manage time is to prioritize your daily activities according to their importance and urgency. There will be activities with high importance and low importance, and there will be activities with high urgency and low urgency. Urgent tasks demand your immediate attention, but whether you give them that attention may or may not matter.

Important tasks matter and not doing them may have grave consequences for you or others. In that case, you will begin with activities that are of high importance and high urgency, followed by high importance but low urgency. The third category will be high urgency but the low importance and if you still have time you can tackle those that are low importance and low urgency.

Delegate responsibilities - This is now as a common sense matter but, for many people, it is not common practice. Some people still want to take all responsibilities themselves while they have assistants to support them. If you are one of those people, it will be good to know that no matter how competent you are, you cannot do everything. Sometimes we take on more than we can handle. Delegation is not a sign of weakness, but a sign of intelligence. Find competent, reliable people and share some of your responsibilities. It will allow you to be less stressed and more productive.

Avoid Procrastination - Procrastination is a very bad habit that can severely affect your productivity. It wastes essential time and energy. The moment you note this habit in you, try hard to suppress it. It could be a huge hindrance to achieving any goals in your career or your personal life.

Use a To Do list - Use your notebook to list all tasks that come to your mind. Make a 'To Do' list before the start of the day, prioritizes those tasks and make sure that they are attainable. For better management of your time, you may think of making three lists; work, home, and personal.

Avoid Stress - When you accept too many tasks beyond your ability to handle them, you create stress. This makes your body tired which affects your productivity. In that regard you have to delegate tasks to your juniors and make sure you have some time for relaxation.

Set up Deadlines - Create a culture of working under deadlines and aim to beat them. For every task set a realistic deadline and stick to it. Remember that when you have no time limit for a task, it will never be done. Reward yourself for meeting a difficult challenge.

Avoid multi-tasking - You may think multitasking is the efficient way to get more things done, but it's not always the most productive or efficient route. Let's face it; our minds work better when we are truly able to focus and concentrate on one thing. Start early; Successful people have one thing in common, they all start their day early in the morning. This gives them time to do more and to follow their morning rituals that help them to organize their mind, time and activities to be attended to within the day.

Reward yourself - Celebrate your accomplishments, however small. This is because we need to enjoy the journey, not the final results alone. Celebrating will boost your morale and equip you with more vigor to move forward. How you celebrate up to you.

Learn to say NO - When you already have too much to chew do not feel shy to say no, politely, though. This will help reduce stress on you and will increase the quality of what you have at hand. You will be happy when you have full control over what happens to you in your day, and the results of your work will improve. Some of the benefits will include; greater productivity and efficiency, a better professional reputation, less stress, increased opportunities for advancement, increased chances to achieve meaningful life and career goals.

There is one more habit that you will need to acquire and hold dear, and that is punctuality. George Washington is an excellent example of a great person who valued time, and his passion for punctuality was born from his youthful study of "The Rules of Civility" noted through his repeated copying of maxims like "Undertake not what you cannot Perform but be Careful to keep your Promise."

"The habit of being prompt once formed extends to everything-meeting friends, paying debts, going to church, reaching and leaving place of business, keeping promises, retiring at night and riding in the morning, going to the lecture and town-meeting, and, indeed, to every relation and act, however trivial it may seem to observers." – William Makepeace Thayer, Tact and Grit, 1882

Surely, if you are serious about yourself, and you want others to take you seriously, then punctuality is not an option for you. This is a soft skill that you have to master and will help you build an excellent image of you for all people you deal with. In a nutshell, punctuality strengthens and reveals your integrity, shows that you are dependable, builds your self-confidence, assumes you are at your best, tells discipline and above all, shows humility and your respect for others.

9

STAY FOCUSED

The key to success is to focus our conscious mind on things we desire not things we fear. **- Brian Tracy -**

If you have your vision written clearly, your goals toward your dream well-set with timelines, and you are passionate and committed to achieving your goals and your dream, then the focus is an important skill that you will need to develop to realize your vision.

Hard-working people focus on the most important goal. Focus requires clarity concerning the desired results and the relative priority of each step that you need to take to achieve those results. When you think of focus, think of a photographer adjusting his lens to keep the critical subject sharp in the center of the picture.

Jack Canfield once said, "successful people maintain a positive focus in life no matter what is going on around them. They stay focused on their past successes rather than their past failures, and on the next action steps they need to take to get them closer to the fulfillment of their goals rather than all the other distractions that life presents to them."

People who experience success know how to concentrate. They realize that they cannot do everything, and they focus on the activities that will give them the highest return on the goals that they want to achieve. They don't believe in the hype of multi-tasking, and they know that the fastest way to finish your to-dos is by doing them one at a time.

Staying focused on your life and your business is all about keeping the important things important. Distractions can sidetrack and even discourage us from staying focused and moving positively forward toward our short-term and long-term goals. Some call it the "Next Shinny Object Syndrome" and honestly, we have all fallen prey to this discouraging syndrome. Nido Qubein nailed it when he said: "Nothing can add more power to your life than concentrating all your energies on a limited set of targets."

The good news is that there are a few simple measures that you can take to help you stay focused on your goals and avoid the "Next Shiny Object Syndrome". By implementing these steps from the outset, you will be more focused, more motivated and more determined. You will soon see that you are making progress towards your goals and so, you will be more likely to stick with them and see them through to completion.

Narrow your list - Avoid working on too many goals at the same time. You will soon see that one goal is distracting you from working on another. You may wish to select one to three primary goals for any given period. These can be on a daily basis, weekly basis or monthly depending on their nature.

The goals should be aligned with your long-term goals so that each day will see you making progress. This ensures that you aren't spreading yourself too thin and, as a result, losing your motivation.

In the process of setting goals, you will find that you come up with a large number of goals. Select the most important goals that you need to work on and put them on a separate list. The remaining goals can be placed on a pending list.

Knowing that these items have been captured for future reference will help you to stay focused on your key goals. From time to time, you may review the 'Pending List' and see if there is any goal to be pulled up to the current goals list. Surprisingly, you will find that over time, you managed to complete some of the items on your pending list, without much effort.

Create shorter goals from Major Goals - As U.S. Army General Creighton Williams Abrams Jr. once said, "when eating an elephant take one bite at a time." Large goals can be very overwhelming, and may eventually de-motivate you. You will feel much less overwhelmed when you create smaller short term goals from a large goal, each with specific, achievable tasks. Instead of focusing on the large goal, you focus on the smaller tasks that you need to complete. This will make the task less daunting and, with each small step completed, you will receive a confidence boost as you note that you are one step closer to your goal. It makes reaching your ultimate goal seem much easier.

Create accountability buddy - If your goal is not too personal or confidential in nature telling people whom you trust about your goal will make you more accountable. Research shows that you'll probably accomplish more if you have someone to whom you are accountable. You could also hire a personal or professional coach to support your goal achievement and accountability.

When you have an accountability partner, you are no longer on your own in your journey. As a result, you will be less likely to allow yourself to lose focus and become distracted.

Evaluate Progress - As the rule of the thumb; the goals you set must always be smart so that progress can be measured from time to time. It is imperative that you know how you are progressing.

As you take action, you can measure your progress and see whether you are making the desired progress or, whether you need to take corrective actions. You may also wish to record in a separate notebook your experiences as you progress with your goals so that you can refer to it the next time you want to achieve a similar goal.

Goal board - It is a common practice these days to walk into an office and find a whiteboard on the wall with some important writing. It will be valuable for you to create something like that to remind you always of your goals.

You could also fill it with images that help you to maintain your enthusiasm and focus. Your brain thinks in terms of images so, if you choose the right pictures, this will serve as both an enjoyable and effective method to stay focused on your goals.

In effect, it gets your subconscious mind "on board" with your plan to reach your goal. You want your entire psyche working with you to achieve your goal. If you want to be truly successful invest in yourself to get the knowledge you need to find your unique factor. When you find it and focus on it and persevere your success will blossom - Sydney Madwed

10

BE FLEXIBLE

Stay committed to your decisions, but stay flexible in your approach.
- Tony Robbins -

Flexible leadership has been defined as the "ability to receive and process diverse and potentially conflicting sources of information, the openness to implement a variety of strategic solutions, and capacity to adapt to changing conditions."

Flexibility is a concept that some have failed to understand because they find it to be contradicting with perseverance. But, in our modern world, changes come fast. As a leader, you might be required to go back to the drawing board and re-evaluate and adjust your goals and find flexible ways to move forward without losing your vision. Tony Robbins says, Stay committed to your decisions, but stay flexible in your approach.

One misconception that ordinary people have about persevering is the notion of staying on a course no matter what. This is true only if the reason for pursuing your goal is still valid. Most successful people became successful doing something different from what they initially intended to do (i.e. Steve Jobs started with computers, went into animation and made his comeback with the iPod).

This is normal because the world is always changing and we know a lot more now than when we started. Successful people know that if their reasons for doing what they are doing changes, there is no point in continuing.

John C. Maxwell, one of the leadership gurus, once said that "Failed plans should not be interpreted as a failed vision. Visions don't change; they are only refined. Plans rarely stay the same and are scrapped or adjusted as needed. Be stubborn about the vision, but flexible with your plan."

The reed that bends will survive the windstorm, while the mighty Oak will crack. The relevance of this saying could not be truer. In recent years we have witnessed many hurricanes hitting various parts of the USA and the aftermath has been fatal and devastating.

Huge buildings have collapsed, simply because they could not bend or swing with the wind. Anything that was capable of bending with the wind did not break, that is the importance of flexibility. This situation is exactly what is being observed in the business world. Changes keep coming every day from all directions. We cannot control these changes, so the only option is being flexible and adaptive to the new normal.

A Strong Character Is Not A Rigid Character, But A Flexible One. You might find this flexibility skill hard to comprehend, but this could be because for many years leaders have been known for their rigid decisions that do not change by outside forces. The world has since moved away from such concepts. Flexibility is key. This is the flexibility of plans not of our dreams. Plans to achieve our vision can be changed several times, but our vision should not change, only adjusted.

In short, a flexible character will be conscious enough to know when they need to be rigid, but a rigid character will probably not be conscious enough to know when they need to be flexible.

Brian Tracy conceptualizes this well in saying, "be clear about your goals but be flexible about the steps necessary to achieve them". Whenever there is a strong reason to review the course of your plane, do so without being discouraged. Flexibility is a new genius.

"The wise adapt themselves to circumstances as water molds itself to the pitcher," - Chinese proverb,

You need to be as adaptive as water. Water never fails; when it is running down the stream and finds an obstacle, it adjusts its route. When you put it in a vessel, it takes the shape of that vessel. When you boil it, it evaporates, when you freeze it, it solidifies. Water never loses, it wins all the time. This is the concept that you will have to internalize in your mind and apply all that you do. When faced with strong obstacles, remember water. If you are truly flexible and go until … there is very little you can't accomplish in your lifetime. - Anthony Robbins.

Flexible people never give up. They constantly change. They constantly adapt. There is no need for them to give up. They keep struggling, adapting, changing, doing whatever it takes until they succeed.

My take is that flexibility is a new normal in today's life. Do not be afraid or discouraged, embrace changes, review your plan, but keep your dream alive.

11

BE CREATIVE

To succeed, one must be creative and persistent.
- John H. Johnson -

When I think of creativity, I cannot help but be reminded of people like Jack Ma the founder of Alibaba Group. His company is about 15 years old now but is one of the largest companies in the world. A person without an IT background but running one of the most sophisticated companies ever. Coming from very humble beginnings, his determination and creativity made a huge difference. Jack Ma never invented new technology, but with his creative mind, he utilized the resources that almost everyone had access to. He said that he never intended to make a lot of money but wanted to make life easy for small and medium size enterprises in China; Global Vision, Local win. The world is becoming very competitive in all aspects of life. Be it for individual professionals or companies.

For an individual professional, to accomplish your goal, creativity has to be at the front of your mind. The labour market is opening up for everyone almost everywhere. Many countries now allow free movement of labor. In that regard, lucrative labour markets become flooded, and competition for available job opportunities is just cutthroat. It is literally survival of the fittest. Creativity in positioning yourself will be important. You may need to specialize or have some additional related qualifications that will give you an edge above the rest. You might be a Certified Public Accountant but also fluent in English and French. An additional foreign language might be the only quality separating you from many others. You may be an Architect with a good IT certificate, or a Lawyer with a finance background, fluent in two international languages. May be an MBA fluent in Mandarin. You need to make a cocktail of competencies for yourself. That is creativity.

Creativity is bound up in our ability to find new ways around old problems -Martin Seligman

If you are a self-employed with a small startup creativity will be your most valuable weapon. In recent years, we have seen small startups that have exploded into gigantic multinational corporations within months. It is creativity at its best. It has only been a few years since I first heard the word Facebook, but look at it now. Companies like Twitter, Instagram, Youtube, and so on, the technology they use is not new, but a just creative way of utilizing existing resources and adding more imagination. The difference is just unimaginable.

You might think creativity is about technology alone, not at all. Creativity is looking into your environment, into what the market needs and understanding how to meet that need with a product that is commercially viable. If you are running a company, whether big or small, you need creative minds to survive. Look at the industry you operate in, make a thorough study of the market needs, the available products and delivery channels. Many times I have noted that, in some sectors, innovation on new products is limited, but delivery channels can create an edge. When DHL started there were our traditional Post corporations all over the world delivering letters and parcels, but DHL and the like capitalized on time and doorstep delivery. People are always ready to pay more if they see added value in a service. If you want to be a successful person you have to be creative. Do not be comfortable with the status quo. Develop a curious mind. Ask questions. Always seek to know what could be an alternative to the normal way or normal product. Could there be a faster and more convenient method of service delivery. Put yourself on the side of the receiver, the customer. What product, or what delivery method could make you happier. Begin today, begin now!! As you walk down the street do not just look at things, observe.

During your conversations with friends and colleagues, listen. They might be talking about an idea that could be turned into a business. Develop a habit of analyzing situations and connect the dots. You might notice a pattern that no one else has noted and that could be a million dollar business idea. Please note that creativity does not have to be only within your area of specialization, not at all. Observations can be made in your living environment or in places you go for business trips or vacations. When Jack Ma went to America, that is when he got to know about the internet, and his business idea clicked in his mind. But he went there for very different reasons.

Edward de Bono said, 'one very important aspect of motivation is the willingness to stop and to look at things that no one else has bothered to look at. This simple process of focusing on things that are normally taken for granted is a powerful source of creativity.'

When Amazon opened operations, within one year, many old, well-established booksellers went out of business. If your company is doing well now, be happy, but not complacent. Keep your mind open and always try to find better ways of serving your current customers or adding new customers. Analyze trends in the market you are in and gauge yourself with your competitors, so that when changes come, you are always prepared and ready to grab opportunities that come with it. Creativity involves breaking out of established patterns in order to look at things in a different way - Edward de Bono

IBM's 2010 Global CEO Study, which surveyed more than 1,500 chief executive officers from 60 countries and 33 industries worldwide, concluded that creativity is now the most important leadership quality for success in business, outweighing competencies such as integrity and global thinking. The CEOs told IBM that today's business environment is volatile, uncertain and increasingly complex. Because of this, the ability to create something that's both novel and appropriate is the top priority.

"Given the pace of change, organizations rise and fall faster than ever before; witness Blockbuster, Nokia and Motorola," said Gerard J. Puccio, department chairman and professor at the International Center for Studies in Creativity at Buffalo State College and co-author of *The Innovative Team: Unleashing Creative Potential for Breakthrough Results.* "So how does an organization survive in such tumultuous times? The same way humans have survived throughout history." Creativity!!

My take on this, if you want to be successful in life, no matter where you are, beginning today, do not just look, observe, do not just hear, listen, do not just follow the normal, ask questions.

12

DEVELOP YOURSELF

Live as if you were to die tomorrow. Learn as if you were to live forever.
- Mahatma Gandhi -

I fell in love with books as soon as I knew how to read. This was when I was around six years old. I was born with a curious mind that made me like to know things and logics and how the society functioned. At a young age, I could read a newspaper and ask my mother what the news was all about. I remember, when I was in grade three, I happened to read a pictorial magazine from China and saw a free subscription sheet, which I filled and sent, and months later started receiving a monthly magazine from China. It was a fascinating experience.

Since you are reading this book now, you must have gone through some formal education, where you were taught structured lessons focused on a particular area of life. Many end up being experts and professionals in their areas, some teachers, doctors, lawyers, bankers, engineers, accountants and so on. You might be one of these or aspiring to become one. Many, after attaining their professional status, do not feel like touching a book. Some say, why read when I am already a Banker, earning a good salary, or an engineer handling big projects, making good money. For those, books make no sense any more. But in this fast changing world, after two, three years without looking at new professional developments in your area, you become obsolete and outdated. The way the business environment changes, all professions and their roles in organizations along with the economy change too. Without creativity, old ways become awful ways. New ways become the new normal. So, if you belong to the group of those whose certificates have gathered dust on the shelves do not be surprised when no new projects are coming your way or no promotions are offered, as the young Tigers pass you by while they climb the corporate ladder.

Your success in life will depend very much on how you equip yourself to face the challenging world. Whether as a self-employed entrepreneur or as a professional working in a corporation, self-development will be important. You will have to continually learn new developments in your profession, learn new methods, theories and practices. This will make you relevant in the current world.

However, for you to have an edge above the rest, you will have to learn some new skills. Skills that will enhance your current productivity, but also skills that will prepare you for taking up bigger and better opportunities that might come your way. And, when you are ready, better opportunities will not only come your way but will rather chase you around.

If you are a lawyer, take a course in finance. If you are an engineer, learn some accounting principles. If you are a doctor, take an MBA course. If you are an accountant, take a law course. And so on. When two professions are merged in you, you become an entirely unique hybrid in the market, and you will be rare sought after commodity. I remember a few days back, in one of my duties, we were to sign a legal contract, worth a few million US dollars, and it was an IT based product.

We had to search around for a lawyer who is also an IT expert. Very few have this combination, but we got one.

So, as you read this, if you are one of those who have not taken any self-improvement opportunities for years, do something. Otherwise, you will become too normal, tasteless like food with no salt. Anthony J. D'Angelo advised that you develop a passion for learning. If you do so, you will never cease to grow.

Successful people keep improving themselves every time they get an **opportunity to do so.** They create the opportunity from within their very busy schedule. Most, if not all, successful people like to read. If you believe that success leaves clues and that you can be successful by thinking and acting like a successful person, then reading should be a part of your daily life.

In his book, *Guide to Greatness*, Robin Sharma, describes Sir. Richard Branson, the founder of Virgin Group, as a person who **can discuss anything with any person.** This says a lot. It is a huge message for you that Richard Branson reads a lot. You might come up with a very good excuses lie, 'am too busy', or 'no time to read'. But could you be busier than Sir. Richard Branson, who owns more than 100 companies, scattered around the world?

Self-improvement does not end with just hard subjects like medicine, architecture, engineering, accounting and the like. Not at all! Self-improvement goes further to focus on polishing up your soft skills because it is the soft skills that you will need most when you climb the corporate ladder, or when you want to successfully run your own business.

It has been researched and observed that reading fiction novels help professionals to sharpen their imagination capabilities and increase creativity. Novels also help people to sharpen their language skills and increase their vocabulary. Read about various topics that have been documented in books and magazines.

Fortunately, there are books about everything. Read to improve how you live your life. When you visit a local bookstore, you will see many books, and I am sure some will catch your attention. Make a plan of reading a certain number of books in one year. You can plan for a book a month. When this habit is well developed, you will internalize it, and you will not stop. It is a good hobby to develop. Through reading, you will know many things that will increase your confidence in public. You will become a leader and success will follow you.

Let me leave you with testimony from one of the leadership gurus in the world, John C. Maxwell, who says, "Pretty early on my own journey; I heard something from the personal development speaker and author Earl Nightingale that changed my life. He said, 'One hour per day of study will put you at the top of your field within three years. Within five years you'll be a national authority. In seven years, you can be one of the best people in the world at what you do.' That was when I made the daily commitment to understanding leadership."

13

DELEGATE DUTIES

*The inability to delegate is one of the biggest problems
I see with managers at all levels.* **- Eli Broad -**

Delegation is one of the most commonly used terminologies in the corporate world. You may have heard about it too. I heard it as soon as I joined a multinational bank just after college in the position of a Financial Controller. When I joined, I had a finance team working under me. The CEO told me that I was responsible for all of the activities of the department; for all that my team would do, and, make sure I meet the report deadlines of the Central Bank and those of the Group Head Office. The CEO said to me, "Delegate the duties to your team, but remain responsible." That was my first day on duty, and delegation was the subject.

After many years in the corporate world and having been involved in many leadership activities, I find that delegation is natural. It is only when it is presented as a corporate jargon that it looks like a monster, big and ugly.

Delegation is natural and indispensable. No one can avoid it. We delegate duties every day in our lives. Our lives require many services in order to run smoothly, and we cannot do these all on our own. We need help from others. And that is the moment that we delegate. When you live with a partner/ spouse, you start delegating duties to each other. May be the wife cooks and the husband fixes something in the house. That is delegation. If one of the parties were not around, those duties would have been done by one person.

We delegate when we take our children to school. As parents, we have a duty to teach our children, and we do, but there are things that we do not know, or we do not have time for, so we have to pass on those duties to those who know. That is delegation. It is the art of letting go when we realize we cannot handle everything ourselves anymore. It is letting go of duty, either because of too many duties on our plate or because of our lack of know-how.

I once read of an example of an elderly shop owner who started the shop during his youth. When asked why he was not expanding by opening another two or three shops which could triple his income, he responded, "I can only be at one place at a time." Meaning he could not trust another person to run the business for him. He could not let go. He could not delegate.

Successful people have the vision to realize and goals to accomplish, so they do not let their ego get on their way. They let go of the duties, not their vision.

If letting go of the duties will quicken the accomplishment of goals and accelerate the realization of their vision, they will do it. They actually do.

If you are an entrepreneur, and you do not delegate, it means your business will not grow. It will be dwarfed. If you are working in a big corporation and do not delegate, you will be overwhelmed with duties and the quality of your work will be impacted badly. You will be stressed and you will either lose your job, your health or your life. Successful people have mastered the art of delegation, and I will share a few with you. But you may wish to study more as you go.

Pass "down" - There are duties in your work that can be handled by any person with a minimum level of understanding and take instruction. If you are running your small business, hire such a person to be an assistant. If you are in a corporation, pass those duties on to your team below. This will give you time to focus on more important duties.

Pass "up" - There are some tasks that require special knowledge and skills. For example; Taxes, Accounting. If your business is small, you may wish to hire consultants to take care of those while you focus on your core activities.

Communicate well - Often delegation goes poorly due to lack of clarity on expected outcomes and timing. The key to successful delegation is being absolutely clear about what you are expecting for the outcome. While delegating, you need to know the capabilities of the person to whom you are delegating.

Empower - Give responsibilities with authority. Delegating provides an opportunity for employees to develop their own skills, knowledge, and abilities.

When you allow workers to make their own decisions, you will ultimately have employees who can work independently, deliver more value to your organization and take up more duties in the future.

Trust others - There is an old mentality still stuck with people, "if you want something done right, do it yourself." If Sir. Richard Branson, now with more than 100 companies, had stuck with that, he would not have made it past his first small company. Let your subordinates work for you while you focus on matters that are most important. What you are supposed to do is simply follow up.

Invest time for long-term success - For the long-term success of your company, delegation is a must. After realizing this, you will need to train your assistants until they master one duty after another.

It can be a painful process in the beginning, but it will be worthwhile in the long run.

Delegation doesn't come naturally to many small-business owners. However, if you want healthy, sustainable businesses and personal life, delegation is a critical art to master.

14

HAVE INTEGRITY

The greatness of a man is not in how much wealth he acquires, but in his integrity and his ability to affect those around him positively. **- Bob Marley -**

Very often we hear people being referred to as, "a person of integrity" and some people with "no integrity." Many have defined integrity as adherence to moral and ethical principles; soundness of moral character; honesty. I say integrity is the quality of being honest and having strong moral principles; moral uprightness. W. Clement Stone made it easier for us by saying, 'Have the courage to say no. Have the courage to face the truth. Do the right thing because it is right. These are the magic keys to living your life with integrity."

The key words in this topic are morals, honesty, and ethics. You want to be successful in your business and your career, but look deep inside and ask yourself, if you are ready to embrace these qualities. Do business guided by your morals in all that you do, stay honest at all times, even if you might be punished, and act all the time ethically, even when it might impact your income.

I can assure you in today's business world you might find obstacles while practicing this. You will be tempted to do unethical acts that seem to have some handsome rewards, and you may think no one will ever know. But I encourage you to never involve yourself in any action that will hurt your integrity. Never compromise your moral principles. Never attempt to act unethically, no matter the tempting rewards that you might gain in short time. Because, after a long time, while you may have forgotten about it, it will come up, and at this time, your business will have grown, and it will tarnish your image, it will cost you dearly, and the price you will pay will be much higher that the gain you received then. Success has no shortcuts.

You might still remember the Enron scandal. It had many details but in its underlying issue was a lack of integrity. The company was making losses; it had lost a lot of money on failed projects but did not disclose that to stakeholders. Instead, they kept reporting profits. They say you can fool all the people for some time, but you cannot fool all the people all the time. And when the truth came to light, investors lost a lot of money; the company became bankrupt, and top managers went to jail. This was an issue of lack of integrity on the party of those entrusted with the company's purse. On the same note, the auditors, Arthur Andersen, had an ethical problem.

They engaged to check the truth of the financial position of the company, and they saw it, or ought to have seen it, but did not report. The audit firm lost the trust of all other clients and was forced to close business. These are the grand scale examples of why integrity is imperative for the sustainable success of your career or business.

Success without integrity is not a success at all. People with integrity keep their word, even when it hurts. Integrity is making values-based decisions, not decisions based on personal gain. No one is perfect, we all make mistakes, but those with integrity are honest enough to admit their mistakes and do what they can to rectify. Mark Twain said, *"Always do right. This will gratify some people and astonish the rest."*

You have to make sure that your living, working, and leading is unquestionable. You have to remember that when you listen to your heart and do the right thing, life becomes simple, and you live in peace. Your actions are now open for everyone to see, and you don't have to worry about hiding anything. Then when you operate with integrity, you gain the trust of other people, especially your colleagues, friends, partners and customers. It is important especially for those in top roles. People will find you dependable and accountable for your actions. Trust develops, and you will gain influence.

Eventually, you will become a role model because integrity is a stamp of ethical leadership. All groups associated with you will want you as their leader because they trust you. My take in this is that success has no shortcuts, the only way to gain sustainable success in your business or career is to wholly embrace integrity. That way, you will gain trust among your colleagues, partners, and customers. That way, business will grow, and sustainable incomes will increase.

Bob Marley said, "The greatness of a man is not in how much wealth he acquires, but in his integrity and his ability to affect those around him positively."

With integrity, you have nothing to fear, since you have nothing to hide. With integrity, you will do the right thing, so you will have no guilt - Zig Ziglar

15

SHARE A SMILE

We shall never know all the good that a simple smile can do.
- Mother Teresa -

Have you ever walked into a restaurant, and all of a sudden you have three smiling faces in front of you, looking you straight in the eyes and welcoming you. It feels so good. It makes you feel like a King. Smiles are powerful because they touch your heart. No wonder they say a smile is infectious. It disarms you.

Some time back, during a corporate training, I was told it takes 12 muscles to smile and 113 muscles to frown. When you smile at another person, a warm, genuine smile, you tell that other person that he or she is attractive, pleasant, likable, safe and secure in your estimation. A single smile is so powerful that it can convert a person with low self-esteem, filled with negativity to a person with a positive attitude.

An experiment was done where men were shown pictures of a woman to rate on a scale of 1 to 10. When the same woman was shown smiling in a different picture, men gave her higher score and thought that she was more attractive.

So, in addition to the mood improvements you will get if you smile often, you will also appear attractive. Almost all people, whether employed in a corporation or self-employed in their own business, have interactions with colleagues, customers, and partners. And if they want to have good relationships with them and make sales to customers, a smile will help them increase the possibility of making that sale.

A smile may be the single most powerful sales tool ever. Why not use it then? Our success depends on how much we sell, be it a physical product, service or expertise.

Even if you are the best consultant in town, you may not seem likable and may be less likely to get a deal, if you do not wear a smile on your face. Because it is business, not war. Why not smile?

It is commonly understood that, if you do not smile, people will not like you. They will be suspicious of your intentions. If they do not like you, they will not trust you. And where there is no trust, there is no relationship. If there is no relationship, there cannot be business.

Your success will be blocked. Imagine how painful it will feel when you realize you missed a valuable business deal just because your competitor smiled and you did not, even though you had better credentials than his.

You might be wondering why people value a smile more than credentials. It is basic psychology. Most decisions are made not on logic, but on emotional connection. Of course, this is after all primary credentials are met. Remember again; a smile is contagious!!

There are many other areas where a smile does magic. You need to know so that you can consciously use it for your success.

Sign of Peace - When you are a leader or in a meeting people will look at you. If they see you happy and smiling, they will feel safe and open for talking or discussion.

But when you are tense and frowning - it creates a primal reaction in others. Their defenses go up. They become protective and guarded.

A smile communicates that you are safe and can be trusted. Great leaders like Nelson Mandela have mastered the art of smiling; no wonder people liked him so much.

The magnet of people - People who smile and laugh a lot are attractive too. The positive energy is contagious. You instinctively smile in response. The world is stressful, so people naturally want to be around people who are happy so that they can be happy too. If you want others to follow you, you can start by smiling more.

It connects - When people smile at each other, they feel connected, even if they do not speak the same language. Is a sign of friendliness that is universally appreciated. It is the quickest way to connect with anyone from any culture. It opens the door, welcomes people into your world, and communicates acceptance. Even if people are frustrated or angry, a smile can often turn them around. At that moment, you forge a connection.

It elevates your mood - Smiling has biological benefits too. They say it has numerous physical and psychological results, including relieving stress, lowering your blood pressure, and boosting your immune system. And it's much cheaper and healthier than taking drugs.

I recommend that you start practicing smiling. Since you may not monitor yourself well, ask your close colleague to monitor you and give, you feedback every day if possible. You have to master this art because it can be costly not to.

A smile is a light in your window that tells others that there is a caring, sharing person inside - Denis Waitley

16

BE RESPONSIBLE

The price of greatness is responsibility.
- Winston Churchill -

Steven Covey says accountability breeds responsibility. He is quite right. While accountability is a sense of being answerable for the results of a certain task, responsibility is the obligation to take on or handle that particular task.

I used to use these two terminologies interchangeably, but they are quite different though very closely intertwined. They are intertwined because you cannot be accountable without responsibility, but you can have responsibility without being accountable.

In the other chapter, we discussed the delegation of responsibilities, but we never discussed the delegation of accountability.

In our day to day conversation, responsibility is used much more frequently than accountability. Many times, the person accountable is the same as the one responsible, or because questions of accountability do not frequently appear until something goes wrong.

One of America's great speakers, Les Brown once said, "if you take responsibility for yourself you will develop the hunger to accomplish your dreams."

This book is about helping you gain a deeper understanding of self-leadership; with an aim to ignite you take responsibility for your success in life. You have to stop thinking that your current boss is responsible for accomplishing your dreams if you have any. It is for you to know your dreams and it is your responsibility to accomplish them, not your boss's, not your spouse's, not your parents'.

Successful people are responsible people. They are committed to their vision. They have planned goals to be accomplished which will lead them towards their dream. These goals are subdivided into short-term duties that align with the goals. Therefore, if you focus on your day to day tasks, goals will be accomplished, and your vision will be realized. You have to adopt this habit too. It is simple.

People will know you are a responsible person when you promise to perform a task, and you do as promised. After they note that, they will like you and trust you as well. They will see you are a dependable person and will want to work with you. If you are working in a corporation, your boss will give you tasks and will give you space to perform them with little or no supervision.

This will boost your confidence and self-esteem, resulting in the receipt of bigger tasks and greater rewards. Being responsible is a trait that can be developed over time, so you do not have to worry if you have not mastered it. With determination, and practice, you can acquire it and internalize it over time. And I will give you some hints because this is why I am writing this book;

Keep your Promises - When you commit to doing something for others, make sure you do it as promised. When you miss something and come up with excuses, others will stop trusting you. If you have never committed to doing something for a community you are in, like a church, family or school, please do, because that is how you will get recognized as an active member and it will teach you to become a responsible person.

Be consistent - When your performance is already at the level that is acceptable, people will always expect the same quality, so you will have to consistently deliver the same good results. However, if your quality keeps swinging up and down, you will lose trust, and you will not be considered dependable. People want assurance.

Own Blames - Be accountable for the results of your work. When results are not good, never try to show that it is the shortcomings of others. When you stop blaming others for your failures, people will see you as a person in control of your life, and that problem will be taken care of. At the end of the day to err is human. Being honest is also a good habit of a good leader.

Stop Complaining - There people who complain about everything and everyone. They just complain. They will complain about the weather, the price of gas, their boss, their colleagues, their spouse, and their children. If you are one of them, you will have to stop. There are things that you cannot change, just accept them and adapt. Dwelling too much in negativity will kill your motivation.

No excuse - When you fail to complete a task or meet the expected standards, be honest, take responsibility and apologize. This will give off the impression that you have learned where you have failed and that you have a plan to rectify your mistakes.

But when you start finding weightless reasons, you will paint a negative image of yourself in the minds of your colleagues. This is because, while performing any task, outside forces will always be there to distract you, and if we were to always entertain them, then nothing would ever be accomplished.

No procrastination - This is an awful disease, try to cure yourself of it now. The medicine will be arranging your daily duties according to their importance and prioritize the most important ones first. Never move to any other tasks outside of your to-do list. Do not go home before your planned duties are done. This way you will conquer procrastination, which will always want you to move your tasks to tomorrow.

Start small - You will have to manage well small tasks before you are assigned to bigger ones. This is because trust is earned, and it takes time for people to trust you. They first need a demonstration of capability. If your boss is not giving you bigger duties, may be it is because you are not handling the small ones very well. It is important for you to build self-confidence.

Once you earn trust, bigger duties will come, and so will greater pay. I believe when you master these tips you will be able to handle your personal goals and any other duties assigned to you. You will earn a lot of trust from your colleagues and progress towards accomplishing your goals will be sustainable.

17

BUILD CHARACTER

*By constant self-discipline and self-control you can
develop greatness of character.* - **Grenville Kleiser** -

"He is a person of good character." Have you not heard that statement before? What picture does it paint in your mind? In 1963, at the Lincoln Memorial in Washington DC, Martin Luther King Jr, in one of the best speeches ever in history, said ". . . I have a dream that my four little children will one day live in a nation where they will not be judged by the color of their skin but by the content of their character.'

The origin of the word 'character' is quite telling. The name comes from the Greek word 'kharakter' meaning "engraved mark," "symbol or imprint on the soul…"

Various dictionaries define character differently but in the same direction. Some define character as "the mental and moral qualities distinctive to an individual." Others say it is "the complex of mental and ethical traits marking a person." or "the stable and distinctive qualities built into an individual's life which determines his or her response regardless of circumstances."

Abraham Lincoln gave a hypothetical example when he said; "character is like a tree and reputation like a shadow. The shadow is what we think of it; the tree is the real thing."

The greatest legacy one can pass on to one's children and grandchildren is not money or other material things accumulated in one's life, but rather a legacy of character and faith - Billy Graham

I can summarize and simplify character as an aggregate of inter-related concepts, including morals, values and prejudices.

A person's character is a combination of such mental tendencies and the way in which he channels them in his daily interactions.

The aggregate of values and morals are mainly responsibility, caring, respect, trustworthiness, fairness, and citizenship. Prejudices are the bad flavors in one's character. A Strong character will have very minimal biases.

That is why people judge your character based on what you say or do or on how you behave or react to various situations in your daily life.

For example, Adolf Hitler had strong prejudices against certain people; that is why he killed them. Julius Nyerere, first President of the United Republic of Tanzania, had a very strong character in all the six pillars, that is why he fought for the independence of Tanzania peacefully, and built a nation that was united and without prejudices of tribalism, religion or color. He fought corruption, and above all, he honestly accepted his weaknesses.

Nelson Mandela, despite being jailed 27 years; did not come out angry, but made peace with everyone, even with those who oppressed him.

A person with good character will always be truthful even if it is not favorable to him. A person with the character quality of tolerance will be more understanding and less prejudice. All this is meant to show you that your character will be critical to your success. Your character can accelerate achievement of your goals or can be a very heavy burden to you that will slow you down.

When you are an employee of a corporation, and your boss criticizes your work, how do you react? Do you focus on understanding the problem and rectifying it or do you whine about it?

When a customer demands better quality service from you, how do you respond? Do you apologize and promise to improve or do you feel your ego has been scratched and tell the customer off?

Abraham Lincoln once said, "Nearly all men can stand adversity, but if you want to test a man's character, give him power."

So if you are a leader, a team leader of two, an employer of three, how do you treat your followers? Do you respect them? Are you honest about your shortcomings? Do you hold prejudices against age, gender, sexuality or religion? Are you a hot-tempered person? How do you feel when others are in pain or trouble? Do you care for the disadvantaged?

You have to know where you stand on every important character element and how you can improve. You have to do a broad examination of yourself, or hire a coach to help you through this process. Check if you have deep entrenched prejudices that need to be uprooted.

At the end of the day, character is who you are. A character can be changed, and can be developed, but it will take strong, deliberate efforts, especially when you are already an adult. Research has shown the best age range to instill the principles of good character in a person is from birth to 12 years.

But also know that your mind can not resist the temptation of accepting information that is regularly presented to it. This means that you can learn or enhance your character qualities if you are willing to make the effort.

Hellen Keller summarized it that, "Character cannot be developed in ease and quiet. Only through experience of trial and suffering can the soul be strengthened, ambition inspired, and success achieved."

18

HONESTY

No legacy is so rich as honesty.
- William Shakespeare -

"The worst thing about being lied to is knowing you are not worth the truth." What a painful and touching statement. It hurts more when that lie came from a person you trusted the most. My definition of honesty is a quality in a person related to straightforwardness, truthfulness, sincerity and based on the absence of lying, cheating and theft.

May be that is why Thomas Jefferson said, Honesty is the first chapter in the book of wisdom. Successful entrepreneurs have strong values, and honesty often tops the list. You can be honest with others and also honest to yourself.

Michelle Obama has said, "the truth matters... that you don't take shortcuts or play by your own set of rules... and success doesn't count unless you earn it fairly and squarely."

The foundation of your success must be honesty. Without honesty, your work of many years can crumble like a house of cards, in one day. When people around you discover that you have been shortchanging them in your dealings, they may not confront you, but will never return to you even if you offer them the best products in town. Business is more than providing quality product or having the best price. Relationships count. It is good to note that honesty is more than not lying, but it is truth telling, truth speaking and truth loving.

Imagine you trust your doctor and he examines you and discovers a certain condition that requires specialized expertise that he does not have, but instead of referring you to the appropriate practitioner, he tries to handle it himself until situation worsens. Do you think you will trust him again after not being honest with you? Probably not.

To be successful as an entrepreneur and in life, you first have, to be honest with yourself. You will have to make realistic judgments about the direction that your company is taking, especially if you are solo. You will have, to be honest with yourself, your capability to offer a certain level of service, your capital strength, the caliber of staff you employ, the size of your office, the culture you want to build and so on.

As an entrepreneur, you will have to be honest with your employees. It will help you to establish a good connection with the people you work with. You may have to embrace qualities like transparency, fairness, and empathy.

When you give a fair comment on their job performance, you will expect an honest response and improvement in performance. If you are caring about what is happening with your staff, they will be loyal, confident and open to say what they really think. Having their honest opinion and giving them yours can improve the results of your work, which is vital to the company's success. Honesty is the fastest way to prevent a mistake from turning into a failure.

Honesty and integrity are absolutely essential for success in life - all areas of life. The really good news is that anyone can develop both honesty and integrity - Zig Ziglar. Since you have a clear vision and goals to lead a successful life then keep it in your mind that everything depends on honesty.

Always tell the people that you deal with the whole truth and nothing but the truth. You cannot build relationships if you mistrust the other party, and vice versa.

You will not follow leaders if you do not trust what they do, and you cannot make good decisions if you are unsure of the accuracy of the information you are presented with. As a result; trust is shattered, reputations are damaged, and everyone is suspicious about everything.

I can testify that living an honest life has made me happy, satisfied and confident. Living free from any fears feels good. You can too, just practice!

19

LEARN TO LISTEN

Listen with the intent to understand, not the intent to reply.
- Stephen Covey -

If there is one thing we can learn from the rise of the social media, it is the intrinsic need for human beings to be heard. The freedom of expression that has always been there suddenly got the appropriate platform. When one has an enormous online following, it is a clear sign that people are listening to what he or she has got to say.

Epictetus, the Greek philosopher, wrote: "We have two ears and one mouth -- for a good reason." God gave you the tools, but it is your choice to use them. We are now in a period where people hear a lot but listen less. Margaret J. Wheatley put it very clearly, "Listening is such a simple act. It requires us to be present, and that takes practice, but we don't have to do anything else. We don't have to advise, or coach, or sound wise. We just have to be willing to sit there and listen."

The art of listening is now an important skill because it is in listening that we get to learn new ideas. When you listen, you get to know what information is useful and what is not.

If you do not listen, it will be like swimming in the sea of information but not getting wet. Very strange! Larry King once said, "I remind myself every morning: Nothing I say this day will teach me anything. So if I am going to learn, I must do it by listening."

I can define listening as the ability to accurately receive and interpret messages in the communication process. It is said that the most basic and powerful way to connect to another person is to listen. Just listen. Perhaps the most important thing we ever give each other is our attention.

Listening is key to all effective communication. Without the ability to listen effectively, messages are easily misunderstood, as communication breaks down, and the sender of the message can easily become frustrated or irritated.

Listening is a sincere form of showing respect to the speaker. In *How to Win Friends and Influence People*, Dale Carnegie quoted a man speaking of Sigmund Freud: "It struck me so forcibly that I shall never forget him. His eyes were mild and genial. His voice was low and kind. His gestures were few. But the attention he gave me, his appreciation of what I said, even when I said it badly, was extraordinary. You've no idea what it meant to be listened to like that."

All successful people, leaders, businesspeople have mastered the art or listening. So if you also want to be great and successful in your life, you have no option but learn and master this noble art.

Ask yourself these questions: Should I be concerned with how people listen to my messages? How can I improve my listening skills? How do I know if people are truly listening to me? Am I listening to them? My emphasis will not mean much if I do not share with you some tips that I use that you can also follow to be a better listener.

Make eye contact - If you make eye contact with the person talking to you, it will give an impression that you care and interested in the message that they are delivering. It is also a sign of respect to the speaker.

Do not interrupt - Interruptions destruct the speaker and may derail him from his intended message. To master the art of listening, you have to freeze any good thoughts that come to mind and give the person time to say everything they need to say.

Often people simply need someone to talk to, not someone who will force themselves in with their own thoughts and opinions. The goal is to shine the spotlight on them, not on you.

Ask questions - Active listening is not about staying quiet 100% of the time. You may ask questions so as to seek clarification or provoke more information so that you can have a good understanding of what the speaker wants to tell you.

Body language - Another great way of showing the speaker that you are following his/her story is by nodding. You may also give some sounds like, "oh!", "ok," "yeah," "mmh," "yes." This means that you are present and actively listening.

Clarify the message - Sometimes you may wish to clarify the message so that you are on the same page with the speaker. You can paraphrase what the speaker has said in your own words and ask if that is in fact what he actually meant. This is best done when the speaker poses.

Validate what you heard - After listening to the speaker, you may not be in agreement with his opinion. However, you are supposed to receive his opinion with enthusiasm and respect. Listening does not mean agreeing with the idea or acting accordingly. In the end, you may offer your opinion on how to move forward.

Do not judge - When you are listening try not to make conclusions before the speaker finishes. Be 100% open minded until the end. Try not to think about other things. You have to work hard because your brain can process 800 words per minute while people can speak 125-150 words per minute. Do not let your mind wander!

Watch the body language - About 60 -75% of communication is body language. That tells a lot about a message. In that regard, you have to understand what the body is communicating to you and match that to his words. Does his body language show trust in you? Is he comfortable with where you are?

Environment - For you to pay full attention to the speaker you must remove all distraction that may divert your attention. Make sure there are no TV or phone noises. Prepare the environment in a way that allows for maximum attention and understanding.

20

LOOK THE PART

My belief is you have one chance to make a first impression.
- Kevin McCarthy -

Making a great first impression is imperative to becoming an influential person. My personal philosophy on clothing has always been to wear great clothes. You never know whom you will meet! Ralph Waldo Emerson said that "what you are, shouts at me so loudly, I cannot hear a word you are saying."

When I listen to that old saying that, "You can't judge a book by its cover" I get a feeling it came from an engineer. Today we have a huge industry of designers specializing in book covers. We now have a huge product packaging design industry because marketers they know people purchase products based on how they look.

We are all aware that career consultants still advise their clients to dress for the job they want, not the job they currently have. They want their customers to gain a nonverbal advantage by already "looking the part."

Your attire is part of your personal brand. This is the most important thing to remember as you get dressed for work each day. What you put on is a reflection of who you are and how you want to be viewed as a professional.

A long time back, I learned about an ancient Greek rule of the first impression which says everything counts. Everything you do or don't do either adds to or takes away from your credibility and your capability to influence someone. Everything counts involve your image or appearance. You have heard it said that you never get a second chance to make a great first impression. Research has proven that, when you first meet a person, he makes a judgment about you in approximately four seconds, and his judgment is finalized mostly within 30 seconds of initial contact.

In a survey of the members of the American Personnel Consultants, three-quarters of those men and women who are responsible for hiring people for big business generally agreed that they made their decision to hire or not to hire a person within 30 seconds of the first meeting. Some other studies have shown that to the large extent, even later exposed facts will not do much to change the conclusions made the first impression.

Your clothes are responsible for 95 percent of the first impression that you make on someone because, in most instances, your clothes cover 95 percent of your body. Your grooming, your hair style and other ways that you can design your appearance from the neck up also exerts inordinate influence on the way that you are perceived, on your ethos with someone. Your accessories, such as purse or briefcase, watch, tie, rings, pens or other elements, all make a statement that will or will not help to place you in a position to influence someone.

In the current corporate world, some have diluted the significance of formal dress code. Some companies do not care about the kind of clothes a staff is in but just puts emphasis on productivity. However, many still know the importance of looking the part and selecting dress according to who they plan to meet that day.

My take is that researchers have come out loud and clear on how the human mind judges upon the first impression. As a person who wants to succeed, you have to learn to position yourself according to your goals. You have to make choices knowing the implications. When you dress well, the message that rings out will be success, confidence, intelligence and trust. But, if you dress inappropriately, your look will be shouting, failure, failure, failure!!

Good grooming is essential and impeccable style is a must. If you don't look the part, no one will want to give you their time or money - Daymond John

21

EMPOWER OTHERS

Leaders become great, not because of their power, but because of their ability to empower others." **- John C. Maxwell -**

Bill Gates put it very clearly in stating that, "as we look ahead into the next century, leaders will be those who empower others." Different people have different definitions of what the term empower means. My notion of empowerment is focused on the transforming or sharing of positive energy or knowledge from one person to another.

Two people can empower each other by sharing knowledge, by teaching each other business or life techniques. A team leader can empower her subordinates, and also subordinates can empower their boss. An entrepreneur can empower her customers and at the same time customers can empower the entrepreneur.

Empowerment, by definition, is about sharing and is not always a one-way route. Sharing is double edged. I find empowering each other is natural because no one knows everything. It is the willingness to share, and the ability to share effectively that makes the difference. The best thing about empowering others is that in the process you empower yourself.

For example, picture a big dark room with ten candles, but only one candle is lit. That candle should be you. You will shine like a star, but one candle is not bright enough to light the room. When you empower other candles by sharing your energy, you light them. Your energy does not decrease, but theirs will increase tremendously, and the room will become nine times brighter. This is how the world is, too big for one person to do much change, but by empowering others, we all become an unstoppable force that can change the world and make it a better place.

Empowering colleagues is the key to building a high-performing team. When you empower teammates by sharing knowledge, by motivating and inspiring them, they will love working with you, and will help you achieve your goals. Your ability to harness the knowledge, energy, and resources of colleagues or friends or customers or partners will be a catalyst to accelerate yourself to accomplish more goals in a far shorter period.

Isabel Allende's message could not have been more eloquently put when she said, "Give, give, give - what is the point of having experience, knowledge or talent if I don't give it away? Of having stories if I don't tell them to others? Of having wealth if I don't share it? I don't intend to be cremated with any of it! It is in giving that I connect with others, with the world and with the divine."

There are three types of people that you want to and need to empower on a regular basis. They are, first of all, the people closest to you: your family, your friends, your spouse and your children. Then your work relationships: your staff, your co-workers, your peers, your colleagues and even your boss. Third, are all the other people that you interact with in your day-to-day life: your customers, your suppliers, your banker, the people with whom you deal in stores, restaurants, airplanes, hotels and everywhere else. In each case, your ability to make them feel good about themselves, to elevate their self-esteem, to make them feel valuable and worthwhile and to make them feel happy to help you, is what will, in turn, make you a more powerful and effective person.

You might be wondering where you start and what do you do to empower people around you in your personal life and your business. I will offer some tips, and I encourage you to keep looking for more.

Share plans & progress - Have you ever been by passed at your workplace? I can assure you it feels terrible and demoralizing. I have learnt that, in the corporate world, it is important to let others around you know what is going on. In your personal life as well, you are advised to share your plans, and inform your closest relatives the goings-on in your life.

Otherwise, it will be hard to get support from them. The same happens in business. Letting your employees know what is happening with your business will make them feel valuable to the company.

Set smart goals - In the corporate world, setting smart goals will be an important part of empowering employees. Giving staff something to strive for will absolutely provide them with a sense belonging and of being an important player on moving towards accomplishing an important goal. Think about how difficult it is to keep hanging around with no direction. When smart goals are set, everyone feels like they are working together for the common good, and everyone can celebrate when a goal is achieved.

Encourage risk-taking - Make people around know that it is OK to fail. Besides, what is life without taking a few risks along the way? This concept applies to both personal and professional undertakings. Risk-taking is what pushes your people out of their comfort zone to discover new horizons. It is through trial and error that knowledge has been gathered, and lives have become better.

Keep your cool - Problems and challenges are guaranteed to occur in your personal and corporate life, it is how you react to them that make the most significant difference. Challenges and problems can be caused by you, your colleagues or outside sources. Learn to be calm when you get bad news and analyze the matter so that your decision making is not influenced by personal emotions but rather by logic. People around should know that you are a confident professional person, and you do not take challenges personally.

Encourage teamwork - Embracing the team spirit will help you, your employees, and your friends and family to feel more empowered about nearly anything.

Before you make a major life decision, share it with a friend and relevant people. It will feel good when you value their input, and they might also reciprocate by giving you valuable direction or support. Asking staff to brainstorm with you to come up with solutions to a problem as a team can be highly beneficial.

Support personal development - Motivating and organizing a suitable environment within which people can learn more about what they do in an organization or even something entirely new is one of the best ways to empower people around you.

Having colleagues or friends who are hungry for knowledge is a great thing, and enabling them to keep moving will be beneficial both to them and to you.

From today on, you should note that successful people empower others by sharing their wealth; which includes knowledge, time, positive energy and may be sponsorship. When you empower others, you eventually empower yourself. To them, and now to you, sharing should be about the legacy you leave behind in this world.

22

LEARN THE ART OF NETWORKING

Networking is an essential part of building wealth.
- Armstrong Williams -

Business Networking is a valuable and effective way to expand your knowledge, to learn from the success of others, to attain new clients and to inform others about your business. I highly recommend business networking as a way to gain new clients and to build a sustainable business.

If you want to be successful, you will find this tool very useful. It will introduce you to an entirely new world. It will enable you to meet people that you never knew you would meet, like-minded people who have ideas that can help you. Individuals who have already gone down the road you are currently on that know the corners and the bumps you might encounter along the way.

Networking happens during gatherings like conferences, meetings, and corporate functions. But also, networking can be done by joining professional or social clubs that have a particular area of focus like Rotary Clubs, Lions Clubs, and the Toastmasters.

While working on a club's activities you get to know people and people get to know you and what you do. Long time back people used to measure one's influence by people they knew, but in the current business world, it is "who knows you."

Adam Small said it well that, "networking is the single most powerful marketing tactic to accelerate and sustain success for any individual or organization!"

I believe effective networking is done face-to-face, building a rapport with someone by looking at them in the eye, leading to a stable connection and foundational trust. Many years back, I joined a Rotary Club, which is a social club for doing community projects in the spirit of service above self. Through it I found myself meeting very influential people in business and public sector. Just being close to them increased my confidence and boosted my self-belief that I can also make it in life.

Eventually, I became a President for my club, and that once again gave me an opportunity to prove to myself that I can lead, and I led people who were far more senior, intelligent and wealthy than me. I belong to Rotary even now, and my network of friends has grown beyond country borders.

If you are a generous person, you can also join a Rotary Club or a Lions Club or any other social club in your city. If you want to become a public speaker or to enhance your public speaking capabilities join clubs like the Toastmasters. If you want to remain focused on business, then join local business associations, or you may try international networks like BNI.

All of these will have a lot to offer in terms of face to face contact with people who could be potential customers, consultants or useful friends. The importance of networking cannot be over emphasized, and its benefits are plenty. I will try to put down a few to help you become clearer and make you more actively involved networker starting today.

Referrals and Business - When you connect with people they trust you and feel obliged to help you succeed. In that case, once they know what you do, they will be happy to refer you to opportunities that they are aware of. And that is the essence of participating in networking activities and join networking groups. The referrals you get here are usually of high quality with a strong possibility of turning into business. So you are getting much higher quality leads from networking than other forms of marketing.

Connections - They say "It's not what you know, but who you know" but I say it is who knows you, what actually counts. This is simply because business opportunities are always given to people known to decision makers. People will not give you a deal because you know them, but because they know you, and have trust in you. Networking provides you with a great source of connections, and really opens the door to talking with highly influential people that you would not have easily connected before.

Free Advice - Having created trust in people you have met at a networking event, it will be easy for you to ask questions on things that they are considered expert on. You will realize that people will be willing to share a lot of knowledge professional or personal that may be very useful to you. In a typical situation, you might have paid for at a consulting firm.

Get Known - They say that, trust takes time. You should be aware that attending only one networking event is not enough. Plan to attend as many networking events as possible so that you keep reconnecting with people you met earlier. This way, they will gain confidence in you as they will have noted your face many times, and they will feel comfortable around you. While you are there, try to offer advice to people who seem to need it. That way, you will build your reputation as a knowledgeable, reliable and supportive person.

Eventually, you will become more likely to get more leads and referrals as you will be the one that pops into their head when they know anybody in need of what you offer.

Positive Influence - People you hang around with and talk to, do influence who you are and what you do, so it is important to surround yourself with positive, uplifting people. This will help you to grow, thrive and become a successful entrepreneur. Networking is great for this. Business owners who use networking are usually people that are always willing to share, with positive energy and empowerment.

Friendship - During these events, naturally there are people that you will meet and find that you share a lot in common you may become closer and begin to share more information on business and personal topics. This is also what networking is all about. Some of my strongest friendships have been started through networking outlets.

Do not be shy, go out and network and start enjoying the benefits that will propel you towards accomplishing your goals and living your dream!

23

COMMUNITY SERVICE

…From everyone who has been given much, much will be required; and to whom they entrusted much, of him they will ask all the more - **Luke 12:48**

I have a feeling that God made me be a natural giver. Thirteen years ago, while in a discussion with one of my board members about the progress of the business of the bank, he mentioned a club where he was a member and the main focus was community service through projects in education, sanitation, environment, health and economic empowerment. Although he mentioned it casually, the idea of serving community, not for money, touched my heart. The following week I started attending Rotary fellowships, and to this day, I am a Rotarian. To me, volunteering fills my heart with satisfaction.

Successful people are generous givers. They know and are convinced of the "secret" that the more you give; the more you receive as long as you are genuine about your gifts.

They operate on the principle embodied by Zig Ziglar's quote, "You will get all you want in life if you help enough other people get what they want."

Myles Munroe said that "The value of life is not in its duration, but in its donation. You are not important because of how long you live, you are important because of how effective you live."

You might be thinking that giving is for those who are already very wealthy, and actually, that notion is very wrong. Giving has nothing to do with the amount of wealth one has, but is more about the willingness to share what we have with those less privileged than ourselves.

In the Holy Bible, Mark 12:43-44; ... Jesus said, "Truly I tell you, this poor widow has put more into the treasury than all the others. They all gave out of their wealth; but she, out of her poverty, put in everything—all she had to live on."

This quote from the Holy Bible touches everyone from all faiths and religions because it is an example that speaks to our situation today. Its point is very clear that; everyone can give something because everyone has been blessed with something that others may not have.

I emphasize that giving back to the community does not have to depend on money alone, not at all. You can volunteer time to offer service that you usually provide for a living. If you are a teacher, you can volunteer to teach about topic that is of interest to a particular group. A doctor can offer free checkups on a particular burning issue in that field. A company can go out and clean a public place where people responsible have not been reaching and so on. There are countless avenues of giving that can make a difference in the community within which you operate.

A few years back, in Dar es Salaam, Tanzania; a fellow Rotarian gave a testimony, on how she and others got overwhelmed by joy and broke into tears when they realized that while implementing a project with people with physical disabilities, they had helped a deaf student to hear her name for the first time in her life.

Mother Theresa said, "We know only too well that what we are doing is nothing more than a drop in the ocean. But if the drop were not there, the ocean would be missing something."

There are many benefits that return to you by giving. Let me share a few;

Public Image - When you give, whether as an individual or a business entity the people you have helped will be happy and will speak well of you. In that regard, more people will know that you are a good community member and will respect you, and if you have a business, its brand recognition will be enhanced.

Customer bonding - some enterprises chose a particular course and involved their customers in supporting it. That way customers will feel that you are their partner in community service and so will be loyal to you.

Choose a relevant cause - you may choose a cause within your area of expertise. Let say; you are a financial consulting firm, and you decide to offer free Tax education to the public. The public will benefit from your initiative, and they will be more aware on their tax obligations. On the other hand, your firm will get good public image, and other people will come for more help, and that will be business for you. I am sure you are now clear that giving back to the community is actually a win-win affair. And so you have more reasons to start giving from today. However small, just give!!

24

HONE YOUR PUBLIC SPEAKING SKILLS

He who wants to persuade should put his trust not in the right argument, but in the right word. The power of sound has always been greater than the power of sense. **- Joseph Conrad -**

Very often I get comments like, "Oh! You are a natural speaker. You speak confidently in public". My response to them is that it is a result practice. To some, I share my horrible first public speaking experiences. I remember my first year in secondary school, which was a Catholic Seminary. I was given a duty to recite the first reading for the Holly Mass. This was just a few weeks after enrolling, so I was still new and not very comfortable yet.

As the time to perform my duty came closer, the pace of my heartbeat began to accelerate. It was pumping so hard; I think the priest next to me, heard it but mistook it for the choir drums. I could feel streams of sweat running down from my armpits. I kept praying to God not faint.

When it was time, I walked to the podium, and the whole church became quiet. The trembling voice that came out of me told the whole story. It was an experience that shook me to the core, and I never thought that one day I would speak to masses and enjoy it. I believe that this is how you might be feeling now the only difference being that I later decided to work on my weaknesses, and maybe you are yet to make that important decision.

Jim Rohn says, "take advantage of every opportunity to practice your communication skills so that when important occasions arise, you will have the gift, the style, the sharpness, the clarity, and the emotions to affect other people." In today's business world, public speaking skills are crucial. You do not have to become CEO to learn such skills. In the corporate world, every person has to be able to present themselves well to colleagues, management, customers and other stakeholders.

Hillary Clinton, now running for President of the USA, also once said that, "if you're not comfortable with public speaking - and nobody starts out comfortable; you have to learn how to be comfortable - practice. I cannot overstate the importance of practicing. Get some close friends or family members to help evaluate you, or somebody at work that you trust."

The fear that overwhelms you is just your imagination. That makes it easy to handle because it involves only one person, and that person is you. Even Robin Sharma, one of the gurus of public speaking, testified that he used to be incredibly afraid of public speaking. He started with five people; then he would speak to 10 people. He later made it up to 75 people, up to 100, and now he speaks to a large group, and it feels similar to talking to you, one-on-one.

Even if you do not intend to become a professional public speaker, skills in presentation are still very crucial for your success; whether you work for a big corporation or are self-employed in small business, whether you are an accountant or a sales executive, whether you are junior officer or a CEO, whether you are a college student or a university lecturer.

Mastering public speaking can be made possible with a strong determination to overcome your self-inflicted fear. There are three ways to overcome this fear; first, is practice, the second is practice, and the third is practice.

It is surprising to note that public speaking is the number one fear in America. Death is, somehow, a distant second. I laughed when I heard this famous Jerry Seinfeld punch line that goes, "this means to the average person, if you have to be at a funeral, you'd rather be in the casket than doing the eulogy."

Let me share with you just five benefits you will get once you master the skill of public speaking. I hope they will be good enough to convince you to make that decision today.

Self-confidence - Mastery of public speaking will increase your self-confidence tremendously. We live in a materialistic world, and a lot of our self-worth and self-esteem is gained by our perceptions of what we think other people think about us.

By mastering this skill, you will be comfortable around people, allowing you to effectively participate in a conversation and make your argument understood.

Public duty - At some point, every person will be given a public commitment that may require him or her to speak. Hence, for you to save face and handle such tasks without fear, learning public speaking skills now is better, while you have time and no pressure. So start defending your dignity now. Skills learned can boost performance in other areas of life

Boost Performance - Public speaking will improve your communication skills, your leadership skills, your confidence and your ability to read and to understand people. Therefore there are multiple other skills you will learn when public speaking that can boost your performance and fulfillment in other areas of your life.

Share knowledge - An opportunity to speak in public gives you a platform to share your knowledge. Since 90%of people will avoid doing so; they will perceive you as an expert in that field. If you use it well, your message will influence many people, and will get you followers.

Promotion - Since many people avoid speaking in public this skill gives you an edge. Since you are the one who can get the message across effectively, top people in any corporation will feel confident with you and will want you closer which will lead to promotion and better pay.

25

SURROUND YOURSELF WITH RIGHT FRIENDS

You are the average of the five people you spend the most time with.
- Jim Rohn -

They say that human beings are social beings. That is why we live in organized families and communities. That is why we maintain relationships between family members and extended family members. Furthermore, we have friends whom we meet in various circumstances. Some friends we meet in school, some in college, workplaces, church and so on.

Researchers have shown that the people close to us influence us a great deal. They influence almost on every aspect of our lives. From our food to our sports, to our studies, our clothes we select. From our faith practices to how we behave and how we want to live our lives. In many ways, we become a cocktail of people around us. If you are an ambitious person who aspires to meet your life goals and live your dream, you have to make and maintain friendships with people who are already there or who are equally ambitious. This will shape your mentality, habits and above all, will support you to stay focused and achieve your goals.

In fact, there is an old proverb that reads, "show me your friends and I'll tell you who you are." I remember when I was young my mother used to bar me from visiting some of my friends. I never understood it then, but I grew up to embrace the concept. They say that from birth to age 12 is the time for building the foundation upon which future education and character will be constructed. But even now, as adults, you should still note that your brain cannot resist the temptation of accepting information that is consistently presented to it. If you surround yourself with negative minded people, you will eventually become negative.

You may have to look deep into your life and list people you spend time with let's say, in one week. List them all and start analyzing their life styles, ambitions, and behaviors. Compare them to yourself. What results do you get? Do they look like people who will help you or will they slow you down? They might be good sociable friends, but if they do not help you to meet your goals, you may have to reduce significantly the amount of time you spend with them. If you have colleagues who are negative, tell them to change. Maybe even stop going for lunch with them. Do not give them your time. Perhaps you cannot run away from your spouse, but if she does not seem to help you, much the best approach will be to share with her your ambitions and make her your accountability partner reminding you to stay focused. If possible help her plan for her vision and life goals.

Go out and search for new friends who will match your requirements. They do not have to be many, around 3 to 5. If they are from different sectors or professions, it will be beneficial to you. The mixture will help you to learn a different set of qualities from various people.

Strong-willed friends can increase your self-control - You must be aware of your weaknesses which are bad habits that you are struggling to get rid of, surrounding yourself with people who possess a high degree of self-discipline can help. 2013, a study published in *Psychological Science* reports that when people are running low on self-control, they often seek out self-disciplined people to boost their willpower. Since self-control is vital to reaching long-term goals, befriending people with willpower could be the secret to success. If you share goals with your friends, they will be like Watchmen for you. When your bad habits want to take control, they will wake you up and support you to get back on track.

Attitude - Friends with positive attitude will influence you also to be positive towards life and to become happy with your situation. As you know, there is no success without happiness. You will never meet your goals if you are not happy. So, especially while you spend a day in an office with stress, it's nice to have friends who will cheer you up and make you feel loved.

Morals - When you have friends who are morally upright, will help you to improve. Friends, who value customers, follow the law, respect their staff, take good care of their families. These are the kind of friends that will help you learn and become a better version of yourself.

Cultural diversity - Successful people are comfortable with people of diverse cultures. Having friends from different cultures helps you to learn how different people live and conduct themselves. This will make you a global citizen who respects humanity and appreciates diversity. Sometimes, we are fed with prejudices by negative friends. When we cultivate diverse friendships, we discover that most of our installed prejudices were blatant lies.

26

TAKE TIME OFF

Rest is not idleness, and to lie sometimes on the grass under trees on a summer's day, listening to the murmur of the water, or watching the clouds float across the sky, is by no means a waste of time. - **John Lubbock** -

After developing a clear vision, knowing that life is short, you should start working on your goals at full speed. They say when wealth is lost it can be recovered when health is lost, you see a doctor you get medicine, and you get well, but when time passes, it can never be recovered. Adding to this fact, we live in a fast-paced world. Everything is made fast: fast food, fast coffee, fast cars, fast trains, fast lane, fast track, and so on. Even if your body were a machine, machines still need some time off to get serviced. So does your body and your mind. You need to rest, relax and recover from life's stresses.

One study observed that "Most people are overwhelmed, but they aren't taking the breaks they've earned. Nearly three-quarters of workers say they are stressed at work, with one in four reporting they are either "very" or "extremely" stressed." The situation is similar in most countries, be they first world or third world, developed or developing. The reality everywhere is that people push themselves so hard to the breaking point.

A little bit of stress is good for you. When just the right amount, that adrenaline rush can power you through a long day at work or boost your workout. While it feels good to conquer the day, in the end, it only feels better and is more beneficial to your health to have some rest, to take a time to unwind and relax.

For your well being, resting and stress reduction are important. While stress can be reduced through daily activities, such as exercise and meditation, vacation can be more effective.

Vacations bring positive impact on your mental health. After a short vacation, even when it is a 24 hours time out, some people experience a better life perspective and are more motivated to achieve their goals.

There are many proven health benefits you will enjoy if you plan your work schedule well and set aside time outside of work to do things that reduce stress on your body and your mind.

Relaxing protects your heart - You have probably heard that stress can seriously increase your risk of high blood pressure, heart attack and other heart-related problems. There are studies to show that stress is comparable to other risk factors that we traditionally think of as major, like hypertension, poor diet and lack of exercise.

Many scientific studies have been carried out, focusing on the benefits of relaxing and almost all have the same conclusions that; relaxing lowers your risk of catching a cold, boosts your memory, reduces your risk of stroke, and keeps you safe from depression.

Relaxing will help you to make better decisions regarding your diet and to maintain a positive demeanor that will improve your relationship with your spouse.

You might be wondering how it could be possible to relax when you have a very hectic work schedule almost every day. You are always busy, torn between office work, family responsibilities, and personal engagements. The truth is that there are techniques that you can apply depending on where you are, what you do and what your life goals are.

Take a Day Off - God rested on the seventh day, why not you? Plan to work for only five or six days per week, and rest completely on the seventh day. Many studies have shown that you will be far more productive in the five or six days that you work if you take one or two days off completely than you ever would be if you worked straight through for seven days.

24hour Shut down from work - When you are off duty, be totally off: Do not catch up on reports, follow up on work progress, prepare proposals, or do anything else that requires mental effort. Simply let your mind relax and get busy doing things with your family and friends. It is important to discipline yourself to shut off your mental gears completely for at least one 24-hour period every seven days.

Short and Long Vacations - Vacations can work wonders on your body and mind. You will meet new people and see new things. Your mind will engage in the discovery of new life perspectives. While away do not try to call home or the office. Minimize your use of TV, phone, and radio.

If you are with your partner, keep yourself engaged with him or her. You should take short vacations every month and one annual vacation upon which you can travel far for a long period. Like go for a safari and see the world's most magnificent ecosystem in the Serengeti or participate in a climb of Mount Kilimanjaro in Tanzania. The beautiful weather and the natural vegetation will make your wonderful relaxation experience.

Take a Walk - Some people say the best time for meditation is when they take a walk. For them, walking pulls all stress away and recharges their mind. If you are one of these people, make a routine of taking long walks to allow your mind to unwind and prepare for another day.

Eat right - Digestion consumes an enormous amount of physical energy. Therefore, if you eat healthy foods like; whole grain products, green vegetables, and fruits, less energy will be required for digestion. Furthermore, if you eat lighter foods, you will feel better and more refreshed afterward.

You might be among people who find the concept of relaxation easier said than done. Often it can be hard to find the time, or you might find that even as you are trying to relax, your brain is racing through all of the different things you have to do. Just know that, like most things, relaxation takes practice. So you will have to practice until you master it. If you find it too difficult to master by yourself, get a coach to assist you or consult a friend who has mastered this art of relaxation.

27

ENJOY LEADERSHIP ROLES

I learned hard lessons, and I've taken that lesson and it's helped me become a better business person and a better leader. **- Rick Scott -**

Ever wonder why some people are always at ease with taking leadership roles? They are almost in five to six different committees of different associations and clubs. They simply cannot help it. For them, leadership is as swimming is for fish.

This brings me to the never-ending discussion of whether leaders are born or made. My response has always been very simple and straight; leaders are born. This is because I know every person is a leader, and I have yet to see a person who was not born. One of the qualities that you need to hone if you want to be a successful person is the skill of leadership. Like I said, we are all born leaders. God put a seed of leadership in every human being's soul. It is just that some have developed their leadership skills while some have not. Simply that! What you should do is let that seed germinate.

A farmer knows for the planted seed to germinate it needs fertile soil, enough water, and all necessary fertilizers. In the same way, that is how you need to let the seed of leadership germinate in you by being ready to share your time, skills, positive energy, and vision. Remove all the weeds of fear, selfishness, jealousy, hate, temper and negativities. Mastery of this skill will open doors for you, and help you accomplish your life goals with a bit of ease. You will realize your dream in a much shorter time. Essential qualities possessed by successful leaders which will help you take charge, motivate others, and make good decisions is that leaders are trustworthy and act with integrity.

Leaders are high achievers who strive for excellence; leaders make others feel important and valued. Leaders are willing to serve others. Leaders are relationship builders, and leaders communicate effectively.

The only way to develop your leadership skills is to practice by taking leadership roles even in small committees. This will give you a platform to practice your theories and perfect them according to your style. When that is done, you will start getting the benefits of being a leader and more leadership roles will keep coming your way. Some of the benefits will be as follows below;

Boosted confidence - Leaders are selected among members of a community, association, club or a group of people with a goal to be accomplished. If you are selected, it means that people around you have confidence in your ability to lead. This will boost your confidence and increase your self-esteem. Your productivity will increase, and happiness will rise.

Hone communication skills - As a leader, you will now have a perfect platform to hone your public speaking skills. This is another essential skill that is fundamental for your life success.

Learn Accountability - As a leader, you will have to carry the responsibility and be accountable for the outcome. You will be working with other members, and you will have to follow through on how the assigned tasks are implemented and make sure they are all accomplished as planned.

Increase networking opportunities - As a leader, you may interact with much more people than an average person on a daily basis. In a leadership role, you will become familiar with other leaders from other groups, and visiting delegations. Building relationships with these people can yield valuable personal and professional contacts.

Sharpen problem-solving skills - As a leader, you will have many obligations; you will increase responsibilities in your life, and you are expected to deal with them all correctly. This will require you to sharpen your problem-solving skills and develop your multi-tasking and delegation abilities.

Gain recognition - When you are the leader of the group, you become the face of the unit to others. You will earn respect not only from the people in your group but also people from other groups will take you seriously as if you were their leader too. Your presence will be recognized even when you are at an event or place not related to your leadership.

To summarize the matter, I am optimistic that you have understood the importance of stepping in front and taking a leadership mantle. Benefits are enormous and are very fulfilling. Let the seed of leadership in you, germinate!

28

BE COURAGEOUS

I learned that courage was not the absence of fear, but the triumph over it. The brave man is not he who does not feel afraid, but he who conquers that fear. **- Nelson Mandela -**

When I think of courage, I think of people like Julius Nyerere and Nelson Mandela. These were great African leaders who fought for independence and equality without fear. Julius Nyerere stood courageously and led a peaceful fight for the independence of Tanganyika (Tanzania). After gaining independence, he supported freedom struggles in African countries, in particular against the apartheid government of South Africa. What he believed was that we could not rest happily while our brothers were still under oppression.

Nelson Mandela stood against the apartheid government of South Africa, and he was ready to die rather than to live in a country where some people discriminate and oppress others. He eventually won and became President after spending 27 years in jail. For Mandela, his most courageous act was not being ready to die fighting, but rather to forgive those people who oppressed him and unfairly imprisoned him for 27 years. That is courage, so solid that you can even touch it.

Nelson Mandela once said, "I learned that courage was not the absence of fear, but the triumph over it. The brave man is not he who does not feel afraid, but he who conquers that fear."

I define courage as the will to do. Courage is vital for you to become a genuinely good leader. To lead your personal life and realize your vision, courage will have to be on gear all the time. Being ready to leave your comfort zone, and paddle through uncharted waters.

As a leader and a person who wants to be successful in life, you have to be courageous. The business world will require you to make decisions and follow your belief. As a business leader, you have to have the courage to change direction. As soon as you notice that your current course is not taking you where you want to go, have the courage to make tough decisions.

Have the courage to fire poor performers because the interest of the company has to come first, have the courage to expand. When you get to the point where things are comfortable, it is easy to decide just to settle in and relax. For you to be that courageous leader, you have to work hard to acquire some crucial traits.

Confront reality head-on - Always seek to know the facts about the state of your organization. This will help you stay on top of what is going on and make informed decisions.

Solicit feedback and listen - Winston Churchill said, "Courage is what it takes to stand up and speak, courage is also what it takes to sit down and listen." Get ready to be told the truth even if it hurts. Truth can breathe new life into your relationships and leadership style if you listen and act.

Say what needs to be said - Sometimes it is good to let your opinion about something in the organization known to people. It may be tough, unpopular and raise tensions between involved parties, but at the end of the day you have put your point across, and you are clear. People may have a different opinion, but they will respect you and know where you stand.

Encourage push-back - You have to know that leaders do not have all the answers. By allowing brainstorming, constructive disagreement, and healthy debate, you reinforce the strength of the team and demonstrate that in the tension of diverse opinions lies a better answer.

Take action on performance issues - Be honest with your staff and let them know what targets they are expected to meet. When it happens that some have failed, you have to take appropriate action, be it reassign or exit. Not taking action could kill the morale of those who are meeting their targets.

Communicate openly and frequently - Make yourself available and adopt an open door policy. Have a communication channel that is easy to understand and allows people to come to you for discussions and clarifications. If you do not have clear responses to a challenge, say so and ask them to look for the proper answer or promise to get back later and do so without fail.

Lead change - Do not protect status quo. Always think of options to make work better, to increase efficiency. Change always will require some adjustments to processes and procedures. You may also require re-allocation of manpower and assets. If your vision is clear, do not be afraid to follow up to the end. Make it clear to your people and involve them accordingly.

Make decisions and move forward - You will encounter situations that will require your decision on an issue that is causing tension. Once you have made a decision on the issue, just focus forward, and do not start analyzing how the other side is feeling.

Give credit to others - A leader works through other people, so when credit is due to pass it to them. They will naturally feel good, and they will respect you more. When blame comes, be ready to take it all. Your subordinates will know that they were to blame, but you did not want them to be blamed directly. Next time they will be careful not to repeat the mistake, and they will be loyal to you because you are ready to stand up for them.

Be accountable: Always perform your duties as expected and follow up on responsibilities you have passed to your people. Expect some people to perform and deliver on their commitments, and have the courage to call them out when they fell short of expectations.

Muhammad Ali once said, "he who is not courageous enough to take risks will accomplish nothing in life" while Jim Hightower said, "the opposite of courage is not cowardice, but conformity. Even a dead fish can go with the flow."

29

GAIN EMOTIONAL INTELLIGENCE

The key to success is to keep growing in all areas of life - mental, emotional, spiritual, as well as physical. **- Julius Erving -**

Emotional intelligence is the ability to monitor accurately and manage your emotions in an intelligent way not to let them affect you or your decision-making process. Emotional intelligence is also the ability to know or to understand the feelings of others to understand the reasons behind their behavior and to be able to communicate better with them.

In fact, many experts now believe that a person's emotional quotient (EQ) may be more important than their intelligence quotient (IQ) and is certainly a better predictor of success, quality of relationships, and overall happiness.

I once read on social media a short story which to me is a good example of emotional intelligence: a parent walks in the hospital with his very ill son and after an initial examination, he is told his son will need to be operated, but the doctor was not around at that time.

Nurses tell the parent that they had contacted the doctor, he will be there soon. The parent waits for 30 minutes, looking at his son lying helpless on the bed he starts to shout at the nurses, complaining about the doctor's lateness. As time passes, the parent becomes agitated and begins to scream at everyone around him threatening to take action. One hour later, the doctor comes, smiles and apologizes and rushes the boy to the theater and after some time the doctor comes out and informs, the still furious, parent that his son is safe now that the tumor has been removed.

The displeased father does not even look at him. The doctor apologizes once again and informs the parent that he has to go because time is up for burial of his daughter. The father could not believe what he had heard!! Having been so harsh, the father apologized. The doctor nods, smile and leave.I find this a classic example of a person who has high emotional intelligence, the doctor, and one with very little emotional intelligence, the parent.

All great leaders have gained mastery of their emotions, and that is why you should also master this quality as it will be very helpful to you personally and to your business life. In our personal life, emotional intelligence is important because it can affect our physical health.

When we become stressed, we need to be aware of the situation and control our reactions. In a normal situation if stress is not well handled it can cause physical harm in our body. Our mental well-being and our attitude towards life are controlled by our emotional intelligence. We can condition ourselves to focus on positivity and avoid anxiety and depression, even when we encounter challenges.

Our relationships - By better understanding and managing our emotions, we can communicate our feelings in a more constructive way. We are also better able to understand and relate to those with who we are in relationship. Understanding the needs, feelings, and responses of those we care about lead to stronger and more fulfilling relationships.

As a leader, you have more reasons to be on top of your emotion management, because in this case, the stakes are much higher.

Self-Awareness - Leaders who have mastered the skill know when they become emotional. This is an important skill because it enables them to understand their weaknesses and strengths. They are also able to read the emotions of the people they are working with. They can note the change of emotions in response to an action or message delivered. In this way, they can craft an understandable message, and deliver it without provoking unintended reactions.

Emotional Management - This is about managing emotions when they are noted. Leaders with high emotional intelligence can regulate themselves and stay in control. As they say, never make a decision when you are furious. It is part of self-awareness and management of reactions. It is vital that individuals in managerial positions keep their emotions in check, as it will help them stay in a respected position.

Effective Communication - When a leader has mastered emotional awareness and management means he is in control of himself and can read his environment. Hence, he can devise a message in a manner that will meet the intended goals. A leader can motivate his people because he understands how to, and then deliver the intended message. Communication is an essential skill for leaders, and it can be a deciding factor in whether or not the team listens.

Social Awareness - Emotional intelligence will help a leader become more caring because he can understand how people feel in a particular situation. If you are a manager in a corporation, you will manage to figure out why your subordinate behaves how they behave. You will be curious to know in case that you do not know. That will help you be in control of how things happen around you. If you are unable to empathize with your employees, you will surely find it difficult to obtain respect or loyalty.

Conflict Resolution - In a workplace, or any other community, conflicts are bound to happen. If handled well it will not be detrimental but if it is not, it can have a negative impact that will affect more people. Skilled leaders are equipped to handle conflicts and provide resolution. With this skill, leaders can quickly calm down any disagreements that arise between employees, customers, and other parties. In conjunction with the above skills, leaders can use their emotional intelligence to develop a more effective workplace.

30

ACT WITH FAIRNESS

Live so that when your children think of fairness, caring, and integrity, they think of you. **- H. Jackson Brown, Jr. -**

Very often in our conversations we hear from people sentences like, "that is not fair." Have you ever asked yourself what being fair is? Well, fairness means, "the quality of making judgments that are free from discrimination."When you are a leader in whatever area: family, company, association, or big corporation and have followers, you are required to be fair in the way you treat them and keep in mind how decisions you make affect them.

When you treat others fairly, your employees will notice and respect you for it. It strengthens their belief that you are treating them fairly and will continue to do so. But also, the other people who you treat fairly will respond in kind. They will give you cooperation, which will make life easy for you and your followers.

A good leader is one who treats everyone fairly not only his employees but also his superiors, his peers, employees in other departments or companies, everyone.

The golden rule - When you are fair, you treat others as you wish they would treat you. In that regard, before talking to people measure your words and speak in a tone that shows respect. Arrogant people are not fair because they do not respect others.

No favorites - A decent leader should regard all his subordinates equal and treat them that way consistently. Allocation of duties should always be in a prescribed manner, meaning there must be job description and rules. Regulations guide decisions.

Don't take advantage - Morals will guide a fair leader. You should not use your authority to mistreat others just because you can get away with it. Never take advantage of a person because you have authority. A leader with no morals cannot be fair.

Follow the rules - A fair leader follows the rules and regulations in all her dealings and will also apply the same standards to herself. When there is no emotional attachment to a person, a leader will be fair by applying the rules consistently.

Change the rules - A fair leader will be ready to modify the rules that seem to be unfair. This should happen not because of a particular person but rather for the benefit of all affected by the said law.

Think about how it affects others - A good leader should always apply his emotional intelligence while making decisions. You will be required to place yourself in the shoes of the other person before making judgments. That will give you an opportunity to give a fair directive.

Be honest - Being fair includes informing all stakeholders about what is going on with the organization. If there are rules, tell them why they were put in place. If there is a new procedure, inform them in advance and explain why the new process has to be followed. If possible involve them in discussions before making some decisions. And be honest with yourself too. Look at why you are doing the things you are and in the way you are doing them. Being consistently fair all the time to everyone is not easy. You will encounter challenges, but if you apply other skills like emotional intelligence you will manage to be fair to a greater extent. Like any other skill, practice will be essential.

Also, you may ask a friend to be your accountability partner to remind you whenever divergence is noted. It is imperative to note that fairness does not in any way mean neutrality. Some leaders find themselves trapped in neutrality while looking for fairness.

Great leaders will make decisions and stand by them. Fair decisions will be taking into consideration the rules, regulations and morals. But when a leader becomes neutral on an issue means she has decided not to act on the matter, and the people involved will remain undecided. It will lead into demoralization and affect the performance of the company.

31

HUMILITY

Do you wish to rise? Begin by descending. You plan a tower that will pierce the clouds? Lay first the foundation of humility. - **Saint Augustine** -

Humility is a word you do not hear very often in leadership circles. Very few, if any, leadership courses include it in their curriculum. It remains a scarce word in boardrooms too. It is as if leadership and humility are opposite to each other. To many, humility gives a vague picture of a weak person, lacking confidence, not sure of herself, not strong enough to stand for her beliefs, and a total pushover.

Preachers refer humility with the example of, "if one slaps your cheek, turn the other". While on the other side, leadership, to many, seems to be about being powerful, physically strong, an excellent orator, commanding, problem solver with answers for any challenge, super smart and a great fighter. Maybe that is where people find a great contradiction between the two skills.

I once heard the former president of South Africa, Thabo Mbeki, explain their original South African culture. One of the core community concepts was 'Ubuntu', meaning, 'I am who we are.' It sounded ironic when you live in the current world. Our minds, from childhood, are conditioned to compete, and the "winner takes all" as Dambisa Moyo would put it. It is becoming harder and harder to trace elements of humility in people with a, 'me first', mentality.

In his book, *The One-Minute Manager*, Ken Blanchard states "people with humility do not think less of themselves, they just think about themselves less."

If you want to be successful, humility is the attitude to develop. I understand it will be a challenging practice to internalize, because everyone around you will be suspicious of what went wrong with you, since the culture that goes by is, 'everyone for himself.'

The mode of life most of us live in tends to make us overly focused on ourselves. We become too selfish, and we forget the needs of the people around us.

Rick Pitino said, "humility is the true key to success. Successful people lose their way at times. They often embrace and overindulge from the fruits of success. Humility halts this arrogance and self-indulging trap. Humble people share the credit and wealth, remaining focused and hungry to continue the journey of success."

Humility does not require you, not to be strong, not to be ambitious, not to follow your dream and accomplish your goals. It does not require you not to be self-confident, not to be a good leader, not to be firm on what you strongly believe in. Humility does not prevent you not to acquire wealth, and live a good life, not at all.

Mahatma Gandhi, one of the greatest leaders in all of history, states: "I claim to be a simple individual liable to err like any other fellow mortal. I own, however, that I have humility enough to confess my errors and to retrace my steps." What humility requires from you is to be strong enough to recognize the boundaries of your capabilities acknowledge your weaknesses and seek help from those who can help. Humility reminds you not to crush others along the way to your success. Not to be arrogant, not to be prideful and brag around because of your success.

John C. Maxwell in one of his books wrote, "some people fail forward. Others fail and quickly spiral downward…The difference is on the inside. It's the spirit of the individual. Those who profit from adversity possess a spirit of humility and are therefore inclined to make the necessary changes needed to learn from their mistakes, failures, and losses. They stand in stark contrast to prideful people who are unwilling to allow adversity to be their teacher and as a result fail to learn."

Development of humility in your life will help you drop your ego and therefore overcome temptations, conflicts and stumbling blocks that come your way so as to help you smoothly sail through to your personal or professional success. Without humility there is very limited growth in leadership no matter how talented you might be, there is no good sustainable relationship with people around you, and there is no respect for others. You will have to be careful with your success because success is like drinking wine, so smooth and sweet at the beginning; it makes you feel happy and relaxed, but as you sip more relaxation overpowers you, and you lose control of yourself, and you misbehave.

When success enters your head and overwhelms you, arrogance takes effect, and pride comes knocking. Respect for others gets evacuated, ears become deaf such that no advice will go through, and you build a strong fortress to make you 'safe' from 'unsuccessful people' and inflate your ego so much that it blocks your sight to reality.

Humility will always keep you down to earth despite all the success you will be getting in your life. You will be humble and always seek to assist others. You will find happiness is seeing others succeed, and you will celebrate their small wins. You will be confident enough to share your secret of success, and humble enough to learn from others, even when they seem much less successful compared to you. Humility will help you understand that there is a drop of greatness in every person.

You can summarize the tips to developing the skill of humility as follows;

» Don't think less of yourself, just think of yourself less.
» Allow yourself to fail, but know it's not the end of the world when you do.
» When mistakes are made, recognize the problem, solve it and move forward with new knowledge.
» Live with the mindset that there is always something to learn from everyone.

As I always say, developing a new skill requires hard work and strong determination, humility is not excluded. But we all know practice is the best way to perfection. Stay humble!!

32

EMBRACE TEAM SPIRIT

Unity is strength... when there is teamwork and collaboration, wonderful things can be achieved. **- Mattie Stepanek -**

Most people like sports, and there are very few if any, which do not involve teams. Even in boxing or golf, there are people behind who work with the player that you see. I am a great soccer fan, and when it comes to team spirit, I cannot help but pull out one example from it.

Just recently I witnessed Lionel Messi, one of the world's most talented soccer superstars from Barcelona, once again making headlines by passing a penalty ball for someone else to score. Messi knew that he could easily score and reach a milestone of scoring 300 goals for Barcelona, but he also knew his teammate needed the goal to complete his hat-trick. Funny enough, the attention did not go to the goal scorer but to Messi, for exhibiting the highest level of the team spirit.

Team spirit is about individuals coming together and bring out their best to achieve a common goal. It is not about giving up your individuality. On the contrary, it is about realizing your potential. It is about bringing your talents to the table and sharing them in pursuit of a common goal. It is about bringing your ideas, your positive energy, your mind, your passion, and your character to leadership and culture.

Team members do not have to be best friends, or even like everyone they are working with. It is about putting personal baggage aside and bringing out your best self and focus on achieving set goals.

Team spirit is crucial for our personal and professional success. In a group of people in which all members are hungry for success, we can expect a high degree of motivation, commitment, and cooperation. There will be high performance, and better results will be guaranteed. This will also result in the satisfaction of team members.

In your way to success, you will find yourself either being a member of a team or leading a team. Both ways you will have to pull out your team spirit to bring your best out or help others perfect their talents to get motivated and committed, so that the team accomplishes the goal as intended.

Companies organize team building sessions. Team building is a process that grows stage by stage from, "forming, storming, norming, performing and later adjourning (mourning). A team will have to go through all these stages to work smoothly and yield results.

Whether you are a leader, or you are a member of a team, it will be good to note qualities that build team spirit;

Shared goal - For a team to achieve an ideal team spirit, members need a strong sense of purpose. They should visualize their future happiness and satisfaction status after achieving the goal. That will create the hunger within them and will energize them to progress towards their goal.

Member competence - Every member should be competent. Members have to deliver at the expected levels. That is why every end of season sports teams purchase new players and let go of those who did not perform at expected levels. Same applies to management teams.

Readiness to cooperate - Cooperation spirit should be high. For a team to work smoothly, every member needs to cooperate with others. Selfishness is a poison to team spirit.

Follow rules - A team coach/leader will always give guidance and procedures on how members will position themselves and what roles they will handle. This will avoid interferences and collisions that may lead to dropping the ball.

Accountability - team members should know that they will be answerable for their results, success or failure. You will note that benefits of a team spirit in any setup are enormous and are much more than what members could achieve individually. No one has all the talents and so working in teams will benefit you and all members. Embrace the team spirit!

33

EAT WELL, LIVE WELL

Physical fitness is not only one of the most important keys to a healthy body, it is the basis of dynamic and creative intellectual activity. **- John F. Kennedy -**

You are what you eat. It is a very short statement and yet very powerful. It is full of message and life. That is why Jim Rohn said, "Take care of your body. It's the only place you have to live."

In this industrialized world, you will find yourself eating the food of which you are unsure what value it is adding to your body, but you take it because you have to. We live in the fast food era, an era of canned foods and bottled drinks. I never thought we would reach a time when water would be bottled and sold. With the speed of environmental pollution, I will not be surprised to come across packs of pure oxygen for sale in streets. China will have a huge market!

Eating healthy has now become a big and important subject. People have turned healthy eating advising into a lucrative career. The number of individuals seeking professional assistance for their diet management keeps increasing as the days go by.

I recently saw a huge headline on the Telegraph in the UK, *"Poor diet kills 70,000 every year, the report says"* I was shocked! This is a huge number by all standards. This is the UK only. What if we got statistics from all over the world? Maybe governments would stop fighting terrorists and start fighting people's mouths.

You have to know that your happiness and your capacity to accomplish your goals to live your dream depends, very much, on what you eat today. In this case, we have to use our emotional intelligence skill to manage the temptation of craving for foods that seem to be delicious but not healthy.

Tony Robbins, one of America's greatest self-help guru, said, "want to learn to eat a lot? Here it is: Eat a little. That way, you will be around long enough to eat a lot."

Benefits of healthy eating cannot be over emphasized. They include but not limited to: You will be more productive, you will be happier, you will be less stressed, you will control your weight, you will eat less, you will think it tastes better, you will age better, you will live longer, and you will save money.

Apart from what foods we consume, our bodies require constant exercises so as to keep fit. I recall a conversation with my former colleague who said we, human beings, suffer a lot from obesity and other related diseases because of eating what we do not need. You amass too much energy and do too little with it.

Naturally, human beings are wired to be gatherers and hunters, where you would walk long distances, climb trees and hills to get food. So your body still functions in that way, even though your lifestyle has changed. To remove all excess energies from your body, constant physical exercise is crucial.

John F. Kennedy also stressed it when he said, "physical fitness is not only one of the most important keys to a healthy body, it is the basis of dynamic and creative intellectual activity."

You need to create a routine like walking some distance every morning or evening. Paula Cole said, "Walking is magic. Can't recommend it highly enough. I read that Plato and Aristotle did much of their brilliant thinking together while ambulating. The movement, the meditation, the health of the blood pumping, and the rhythm of footsteps... this is a primal way to connect with one's deeper self." There are many physical exercises that you can do at home, and you will not need to go to the gym.

Exercises like aerobics, rope skipping, push-ups and various body stretching exercises. These are very effective when done efficiently and always. Physical exercises are important for people of all ages and status, young and old, male and female, healthy and overweight. Benefits of physical exercises are many, physical and psychological;-

Mental Wellness - Exercise is one of the best ways to manage stress and depression and make you feel good. Some people think better while they are exercising. That is the time their brains are clear of all other distractions.

Physical wellness - Exercises will strengthen your muscles and increase your endurance. This makes your body capable of handling any duty that may arise.

Psychological wellness - When your body is fit your confidence is boosted along with your self-esteem. You like your body and feel good about it. The discipline that you develop will also help you in performing your duties. My take is that exercise and physical activity will make you boost your mental feeling, gain health benefits and have fun.

As a general goal, plan for at least 30 minutes of physical activity every day. If you want to lose weight or meet specific fitness goals, you may need to exercise more. Check with a doctor before starting a new exercise program, especially if you have not exercised for a long time, or if you have chronic health problems, such as heart disease, diabetes, arthritis or if you do not feel well. Eat Well, Live Well!!

34

EMBRACE EXCELLENCE

*The will to win, the desire to succeed, the urge to reach your
full potential... these are the keys that will unlock the door
to personal excellence.* **- Confucius -**

Excellence is not a skill; it is an attitude. It is an attitude of always striving for the best, to be the best, do the best and have the best. It is not easy to be the best in everything, but you can choose to be the best in one area that you love. It is said that the quality of a person's life is in direct proportion to their commitment to excellence, regardless of their chosen field of endeavor. Excellence is not static, when you achieve it then it is all over, not at all. It is a continuous endeavor always to be better today than you were yesterday.

To an average person this is too much and over stretching, but to you, who wants to be successful in this competitive world, excellence is a must. Not negotiable. Desire is the key to motivation, but it is determination and commitment to an unrelenting pursuit of your goal, a commitment to excellence, that will enable you to attain the success you seek.

Vince Lombardi was correct when he said that, "Perfection is not attainable, but if we chase perfection we can catch excellence."

The world has developed to where it is now, not because of average people, but people who live and dream excellence. Those are the people who love what they do such that excellence for them is not an option but a way of life. The great Chinese philosopher, Confucius, said, "the will to win, the desire to succeed, the urge to reach your full potential… these are the keys that will unlock the door to personal excellence."

Steve Jobs said, "be a yardstick of quality. Some people aren't used to an environment where excellence is expected." Steve Jobs is an example of an individual who was determined for nothing else but excellence. The tools he created before his death, and the standard of quality he left is what is driving his company to date, and the whole industry worldwide is working to catch up.

There are many people like, Michelangelo, one of the greatest sculptor, painter, and architect, whose work is still unparalleled 500 years later. Other individuals who attained excellence, to mention but a few, are like Pablo Picasso, Michael Jordan, Pele, and Christiano Ronaldo.

Excellence comes when you decide to be the best at what you do. Be the best in your community, the best in your company, industry, be the best in the whole country and one of the best in the world.

Aristotle once said that "Excellence is an art won by training and habituation. We do not act rightly because we have virtue of excellence, but we rather have virtue of excellence because we have acted rightly. We are what we repeatedly do. Excellence, then, is not an act but a habit." To be the best you have to have an inner determination to be the best. There some key mental principals that will lead you to excellence.

Create hunger for excellence - You have to a have a deep desire for excellence, in a field that you love, something that you feel happy doing. Set the goal yourself not because someone wants you to, because when the going gets tough, you might think of abandoning the cause. It does not make sense to sign yourself up for something and put in a half-baked effort.

Benchmark against the best - What is it you are working on? What is your field of operation? Who are the people who are the best in this area? What are the results they have achieved? Set your targets to the same level as their best results, or even higher if you are feeling up to it.

Believe in your ability - Self-confidence is the beginning of your success. When you believe in yourself, that is when others will believe in you. You need to be confident. Starting where you are will make you gather confidence once you start achieving small wins, or improvements. The rule is, bite by bite, you finish the elephant.

Build concrete strategy & plans - After having a clear dream, you have set goals that will make you achieve your dream. You will need a plan to guide you to start walking towards the goal. These will be small milestones and types of activities to do or participate in, or investments to make, or skills to acquire.

Learn from the best - You must get yourself a mentor or a coach. These will be people who know the techniques of the industry.

They will speed up your learning process and also inspire you to be like them or even beat them. If you cannot find mentors easily, then read books on your topic. Sometimes books are better because they give you distilled information.

Try various methods - When you have your dream clear and your goal, you can use any plan that can help you reach your goal. Do not limit yourself to only one plan. Be open to possibilities that might be better than what you started with. The focus is your goals, excellence. That is what you want to achieve.

Go all out and Work hard - Start out knowing that the journey to excellence will not be easy at all. But also know that hard work pays off. Look at every successful person in the world; they work more than their peers. If you want excellence, you will be among top 5% of the people in the world, which means you must be willing to do what those top 5% do. And that is getting crazily focused at your ambition. Put in the hours. Remove from your life any activities that are time-consuming but not adding value. Drop them and invest more time on your goal.

Focus your efforts - They say one who chases two rabbits catches none. Focus your energy on few goals, 2 or 3. This will help you have a greater impact that working on too many goals at the same time and end up not getting the best results. Keep your to-do list and pending list, so that when one activity is finished you know which one follows. Start with the most important goals then go down the list.

Be flexible - The only thing that is constant in life is change. For you to achieve excellence, you will have to be flexible. Flexibility does not require you to change your plans but adjust them so that they work according to the current environment. It is a fast world, so things happen fast, and so does change. Do not be afraid of change, be willing and try to anticipate it.

Never give up - There is no failure except in no longer trying. Remember what you want is excellence in what you are doing already. Colin Powell said, "success is the result of perfection, hard work, learning from failure, loyalty, and persistence. So when you seem to be failing do not give up, learn from the experience and keep moving."

35

SET MEDITATION TIME

Meditation makes the entire nervous system go into a field of coherence.
- Deepak Chopra -

The first time in my life I encountered meditation was when I joined a Catholic seminary. I was around 12 years old then. Just a few hours after arriving at the school, the bell rang, and we went for afternoon meditation. The church became so quiet that I could hear the sound of my breathing. I was later told meditation was a time to get in touch with your soul.

Hugh Jackman said, "meditation is all about the pursuit of nothingness. It's like the ultimate rest. It's better than the best sleep you've ever had. It's a quieting of the mind. It sharpens everything, especially your appreciation of your surroundings. It keeps life fresh."

In today's stressful world where we have hectic work schedules and lot of responsibilities; work, family, personal and social we cannot escape feeling stressed. To recharge our inner energy and relieve all stress from our mind, we need to dedicate some time either daily or weekly to help your mind detoxicate.

That is meditation. They say, what physical exercise does to our body muscle, which is what meditation does to our mind. It lets us draw some power from the eternal source.

Gurudev Sri Ravi Shankar in *The Art of Living* says, "meditation is that which gives you deep rest. The rest in meditation is deeper than the deepest sleep that you can ever have. When the mind becomes free from agitation, is calm and serene and at peace, meditation happens."

The benefits of meditation are many. It is an essential practice for mental hygiene. A calm mind, good concentration, clarity of perception, improvement in communication, blossoming of skills and talents, an unshakeable inner strength, healing, the ability to connect to an inner source of energy, relaxation, rejuvenation, and good luck are all natural results of meditating regularly.

In today's world where stress catches on faster than the eye can see, or the mind can perceive, meditation is no more a luxury. It is a necessity. To be unconditionally happy and to have peace of mind, we need to tap into the power of meditation.

Practice meditation regularly. Meditation leads to eternal bliss. Therefore meditate, meditate, and meditate. You can practice meditation on your own by just getting into nice quiet place, sit (anyhow) and observe your chest, shoulders, rib cage and belly.

Make no effort to control your breath; simply focus your attention. If your mind wanders, simply return your focus back to your breath. Maintain this meditation practice for 2–3 minutes to start, and then try it for longer periods.

An eight-week study conducted by Harvard researchers at Massachusetts General Hospital (MGH) determined that meditation literally rebuilds the brains grey matter in just eight weeks. It's the **very** first study to document that meditation produces changes over time in the brain's grey matter.

Grey matter is known to be important for learning and memory and in structures associated with self-awareness, compassion, and introspection.

Although the concept of meditation might be new to you, it is worthy practicing, and it will help you become better, feel better and improve your well-being and performance. Study it more and keep practicing. Remember practice makes perfect!

36

LEARN PUBLIC MANNERS

Good manners will open doors that the best education cannot.
- Clarence Thomas -

We live in an image driven century. People will grade you and value you according to how you behave in public. They will not know whether you had straight A's in college or you are a super talented accountant. Naturally, we like to be associated with well-behaved people. In corporations, those who behave themselves well in public and at their workplace have a much higher possibility of getting promoted, because they represent the image of the company well.

The fact is, all corporations, employers, employees, clients or partners are in there to become successful and so public manners are of high importance to all. Those with good public manners are perceived to be confident, respectful and responsible, and they will attract others to like to work with them, do business together. They say Good manners will open doors that the best education cannot, and I cannot agree with them more. Most manners are universal, and so wherever you are in the world, the same manners will apply. Mostly public manners are acquired at a young age.

Parents would teach you how to behave in public. Manners like; Treat everyone with kindness and respect. Don't stare or make fun of anyone, no matter how strange they may look. Put litter in its place. Say you are sorry if you bump into someone or accidentally step on someone's toe. Remember to say please and thank you.

Do not walk in bunches so that you block others. If you need to stop and talk, move over to the side away from the flow of traffic. Manners are an integral part of civilization. They are unwritten acceptable codes of conduct. Manners help the society to run smoothly in peace. Have you ever imagined without public manners how chaotic our cities would be? Life would be unbearable, and business would not move.

Some have categorized them into different groups, like family manners, social (public manners), office manners and table manners. All are important, and you need to learn them to have a better relationship with your family, friends, colleagues, clients and all people you meet. Manners will open doors for your success. These days the trend is more business is conducted over the dining table in executive dining rooms, homes, clubs, and restaurants. Business is increasingly becoming relationship based more than just product quality and price base. It is essential that you, as the business professional, feel confident and comfortable at a dining table, by learning the table etiquette.

Remember that good self-presentation at the dining table could help you, develop strong client relationships, increase sales, improve self-image, exert confident professionalism, close the deal, secure a new job or promotion and make a positive and lasting impression.

If you have employees under you, it is better to put down standard office etiquette to avoid behaviors that could cause misunderstanding and jeopardize tranquility of the working environment. It is important to note that manners and etiquette are a bit different. As I mentioned earlier, manners are universal, but etiquette varies from culture to culture. Etiquette follows traditions of a particular place.

For example, being polite to people is universal, waiting on a queue is universal, not to litter a public place in universal. One example of business etiquette is that Chinese business people often greet a person by offering a business card while western people great by offering a handshake, while Japanese business people do not shake hands.

When you travel for business, it will be important to research business etiquette of the place you are traveling to avoid embarrassments and potentially even lose business. Also remember, wearing the correct dress for any occasion is a matter of good manners.

Business is becoming more global, and the world is becoming more of a village. Knowing how to behave at every particular moment will help you avoid unnecessary obstacles towards achieving your goal. The rule is simple, keep learning and practicing until you master it.

37

PRACTICE EMPATHY

In a high-IQ job pool, soft skills like discipline, drive and empathy mark those who emerge as outstanding. **- Daniel Goleman -**

I recently sat on an interviewing panel for a new organization that is hiring people to kick start its operations. We met very intelligent people some from big corporations who wanted to move to our company because they wanted career growth. But one gentleman told us that he wanted to move not because of the salary, not because of workload or work stress, but he wanted to move because his boss was treating employees like machines.

He went on to say that what the boss wanted was numbers only; he did not care whether an employee was sick, or other personal challenges. He said the boss shouts at employees in front of customers and does not have the courtesy to understand reasons for perceived problem. No amount of salary will keep people at your office if they feel you do not care about them or their feelings. In his book, *A Whole New Mind: Moving from the Information Age to the Conceptual Age*, Daniel Pink predicts that power will reside with those who have strong right-brain (interpersonal) qualities.

In a popular Harvard Business Review article entitled *"What Makes a Leader?"*, Dr. Daniel Goleman isolates three reasons why empathy is so important, "the increasing use of teams, (which he refers to as "cauldrons of bubbling emotions"), the rapid pace of globalization (with cross-cultural communication easily leading to misunderstandings) and the growing need to retain talent." Goleman continues to say "leaders with empathy,...do more than sympathize with people around them, they use their knowledge to improve their companies in subtle, but important ways." This doesn't mean that they agree with everyone's view or try to please everybody. Rather, they "thoughtfully consider employees' feelings, along with other factors, in the process of making intelligent decisions."

There are many interpersonal qualities that a leader, manager, supervisor or any other person needs to have, and one of them is empathy. Daniel Pink says empathy is about standing in someone else's shoes, feeling with her heart, seeing with her eyes. Not only is empathy hard to outsource and automate, but it makes the world a better place. Empathy is more than simple sympathy, which is being able to understand and support others with compassion or sensitivity.

As a leader, team leader, manager, supervisor or an individual, if your emotional abilities are not in hand, if you do not have self-awareness, if you are not able to manage your distressing emotions, if you cannot have empathy and have effective relationships, then no matter how smart you are, you are not going to get very far.

When empathy is practiced at workplaces, it shows deep respect for co-workers and gives an impression that you care, as opposed to just going by rules and regulations. An empathic leader makes everyone around him feel confident, and as a valued team member, which increases productivity, morale, and loyalty. Empathy is always handy of a well-liked and respected leader.

Stephen Covey, author of, *7 Habits of Highly Effective People*, wrote, "when you show deep empathy toward others, their defensive energy goes down, and positive energy replaces it. That's when you can get more creative in solving problems."

In *Leaders Eat Last*, Simon Sinek says great leaders, "prioritize the well-being of their people and, in return, their people give everything they've got to protect and advance the well-being of one another and the organization."

To be a successful leader and cement your relationship with the people working around you, development of empathy will be essential. You can start by developing a relationship with your people, which will help you understand them and build trust.

Another tip will be listening attentively to what people are saying. Active listening will help you learn their body language which also tells a lot. This will help you to understand the difficulties others face, all of which helps to give your people a good feeling of being heard and recognized.

I look at empathy as a lubricant in an engine of the car. It can be a posh car but with low lubricant, the engine will not work properly and may crush. It is in the same way for your team; you can build a big company with a lot of resources, but if empathy is low, performance will be low too. The bottom line is that empathy is paramount; mastering it will require practice and constant learning.

Always remember what Theodore Roosevelt said, "Nobody cares how much you know until they know how much you care."

38

PERSEVERE THROUGH CHALLENGES

Great works are performed not by strength but by perseverance.
- Samuel Johnson -

What is perseverance? I look at it as the ability to keep on keeping on, even when our efforts are met with disappointment or failure, it is an ability that can make all the difference in the world. Perseverance is also a personal value because it gives shape and strengthens your character which allows you to keep your focus on your goal.

Most of the important things in the world have been accomplished by people who had kept on trying even when there seemed to be no hope at all. They persevere on their course until they find a breakthrough. When you set your goals and start working on your plan know for sure it will not be easy to accomplish it unless you have set for yourself a very low goal. But if your goal is big enough to scare you then you will need to persevere to attain it.

The Sylvester Stallone's rags-to-riches story of how he overcame overwhelming odds in his life to be the international movie star we know him to be today.

When he was a baby, he was born with a half-paralyzed face due to birth complications, which led to having an impaired speech. Because of this, he was rejected many times by casting agents, but he never gave up. He finally got his big break as the star of Rocky – and this only came after years and years of relentlessly trying. When Michael Jordan was in his sophomore year, he tried out for the varsity basketball team but was rejected by the coach for being too short!

Being left out of the team at first devastated him but he accepted the rejection as a challenge and strove to improve his technique and playing style to overcome for his "lack." This spirit of dedication to improvement and that failure should only lead to success is the belief and idea that Michael Jordan based his sports career on.

He once said, "I've missed more than 9000 shots in my career. I've lost almost 300 games. 26 times I've been trusted to take the winning shot and missed. I've failed over and over and over again in my life. And that is why I succeed."

If you listen to personal stories of all successful people, you will learn the common attribute is perseverance. Success never comes easy. Easy money, easy success is never success at all, because it is usually short-lived and often comes through compromised morals.

Walter Elliot said, "Perseverance is not a long race, it is many short races one after the other."

Positive psychology leader Martin Seligman found in his research that the difference between people who give up when faced with difficulties and the ones who keep on keeping on is how they think of good and bad events. Optimists see negative events as temporary and will learn from it so that they can do better next time. Pessimists, on the other hand, see negative events as set in stone and affecting everything.

Your perseverance and continued progress towards your goal, you will get you other psychological and social benefits. Perseverance builds trust in you from the people who know how you finally triumphed against odds.

Next time they work with you, they will be aware that you are not a quitter. It increases your sense of self-worth to take full ownership of the goal you set out to achieve. You accept that your destiny is in your hands.

The fact that you remained committed to the goal, the way you value that goal becomes much higher than before and heightens your motivation.

In the process of moving on to achieve your goal against obstacles, you learn more about yourself because you have been tested at different levels than ever before. You also learn new techniques about the sector you work in.

The former President of India, Abdul Kalam once said, "never stop fighting until you arrive at your destined place, that is, the unique you. Have an aim in life, continuously acquire knowledge, work hard, and have the perseverance to realize the great life."

39

WALK THE TALK

People may doubt what you say, but they will believe what you do.
- Lewis Cass -

"Do it as I say" style of leadership belongs to out of touch leaders who believe being a leader is about issuing commands from their swinging chairs. This is a dictatorial type where a leader is assumed to have all the answers, and subordinates are not allowed to think but follow orders.

That might have worked in the early 20th century, but in the current business world, leaders have to lead from the front. They have to show examples of what they want followers to do. They have to walk the talk.

Ever heard of the boss who tells everyone to be at work on time, but he is never on time in office and is always late for important meetings, or a manager who criticizes everyone for spending time on the Internet, but is seen busy on social media in the middle of the afternoon. Situations like these destroy the morale of staff, who becomes demoralized, and they will work just to meet minimum standards not to get fired.

Mahatma Gandhi said, "we must become the change we want to see." He preached about nonviolence mode of fighting against oppression and lived it until his death. People followed him and believed in his world because he participated in the movements himself, not just preaching for others to act. This is the century of, "do as I do and not do as I say"." It makes more sense and motivates followers that the leader truly believes in what he says because he lives the idea himself or herself. When an organization has put in policies, values, and procedures, all are expected to follow to the dot, including the CEO.

"Organizations have to have values. But so do people. To be effective in an organization, one's values must be compatible with the organization's values. They do not need to be the same. But they must be close enough so that they can coexist." – Peter Drucker.

Nelson Mandela is probably the most iconic person of the 21st century for his leading the fight towards abolishment of apartheid in South Africa. He fought in courtrooms as a lawyer; he fought in streets, he fought from the bush, went to jail for 27 years and said he would rather die than live under oppression. He came out and fought for democracy and became president. Hundreds of people perished in the process, but the rest did not give up. They knew they had a strong leader, who walked the talk!

Walking the talk also includes, meaning what you say, and saying what you mean. Keep your word. When you have integrity, you are trusted, whatever you say; people will believe totally. This trust can only be earned. Earned by always keeping your promises.

Walking the talk also means saying the truth, nothing but the truth. You should never lie, no matter what the impact will be. Tell the truth even if you will be punished for it. The habit of saying so called, 'white lie' leads to denting your integrity. Be impeccable with your word.

If you want to be truly successful as a leader, walking the talk is not an option. You have to embrace the, 'do as I do' mentality and not 'do as I say'. You have to lead from the front!

John F. Kennedy said that "as we express our gratitude, we must never forget that the highest appreciation is not to utter words, but to live by them."

40

HAVE FUN AT WORK

If I quit having fun, then it's time for me to quit working.
- Charlaine Harris -

Having fun in a working environment can have many faces and can affect the performance of the organization in many positive ways. One of my former employers had an excellent arrangement, where once a year, we had a community day. All employees would group themselves whether by department or as they wish, plan on what community event they would like to do, and we would present our budgets and on the community day we would go and do it ourselves. I remember it was one of the best arrangements.

What made it different is that the activities were all arranged by group members, and so we would always select communities that we felt needed us the most. That used to be one of the most fulfilling activities, full of fun. When you lead your organization, try to create an environment where staff can feel happy and work hard at the same time.

When people have fun they interact well, communication becomes easier and performance increases. I have observed that for many companies the only time they have fun is the so called staff day or end of year party. While that is important, day to day fun at workplace goes a long way.

For staff, meeting their performance targets is already very stressful, so if environment is not helping staff to calm down, then it can be a source of health problems. I remember a case in a certain organization a colleague collapsed in the restroom after she had had a harsh meeting with her boss. While she expected a little appreciation for her improving performance, instead she was harshly criticized for not meeting her targets.

When employees are having fun in the office, they relax and open up, and it becomes easy for a leader to understand them better. Staff will feel confident to share their personal realities as well as seek help when necessary.

As a leader, you should remember that staff spend almost three-quarters of their active life in the office. So the office is like a second home. You have to make it as pleasant as possible. Some people can perform better when they are having a bit of fun at their workplaces. Author Dave Hemsath in the book *"301 Ways to Have Fun at Work,"* also goes on to say that he believes fun may be the single most important trait of a highly effective and successful organization.

Having 'fun' to some leaders brings a very bad taste. Their perception of having fun is chaos, laziness, staff talking whole day, lack of work discipline and performance would nose dive instantaneously.

Never underestimate the importance of having fun. Because when you have confidence, you can have a lot of fun. And when you have fun, you can do amazing things. We all know people rarely succeed unless they have fun in what they are doing. Having fun should not be only limited to staff, but can be extended to customers as well. I worked with a boss who knew very well how to entertain customers and those we were targeting. When clients come with their request for sponsorships, he would go all the way to offer more and give ideas on how to make their event much bigger and better than they ever imagined. That was his genius. Customers would have a lot of fun, and the bond would strengthen and eventually do more business.

When staff are happy, having fun at work, they will perform better, and they will not like to move to another company. And when customers are enjoying the relationship with your company they will be loyal and will attract their partners also to do business with you.

So if you are a team leader, manager, CEO just ask yourself if your people around are having fun. Ask yourself whether they are having fun by themselves or you also are having fun with them.

Have you created an environment allowing them to have fun while meeting their work targets? Plan to also have fun with clients, let it not be for relationship managers or marketing people only, but the whole company including you. Are you one of those leaders who think sharing a joke with staff will dilute your authority?

41

KICK AWAY BAD HABITS

The only proper way to eliminate bad habits is to replace them with good ones. **- Jerome Hines -**

Every person has bad habits. That is part of our nature, as human beings. It does not matter if you are the president, a cabinet minister, CEO, manager junior officer, student or anybody; we all have habits that need improvements. The difference comes where successful people know their limitations and weaknesses and work to improve them.

Also, successful people focus their energy on areas that they have strength and capitalize to accomplish their goals. They also put a plan in place to get rid of bad habits or keep improving on the good ones.

Habits are defined as acquired behavior or thought pattern that you have repeated so many times that it has become almost unconscious. As you likely already know, habits can be both helpful and harmful. The good thing about habits is that they are automatic, and so do not require our attention or energy. This frees our brain to focus our energy on other important activities.

When we have good habits, like arriving at work on time or being optimistic, we create a positive, ingrained forward motion that we don't have to think about. The same happens to bad habit; we engage in them unknowingly, and they can damage our personal lives and careers without us being aware of them.

If you are working hard to be successful and leave a good impression on the people you touch, focus on fighting the bad habits first, as you internalize their corresponding good habits, your life is going to snowball into a never-ending quest for improvement. The good news is that you can start today.

Developing good habits and changing the bad ones, of course, goes hand in hand with success. There is no 'ifs' or 'buts' in this; it is imperative to create solid habits that jell with your values for you to succeed in your field of interest.

But to know all habits that might hold you back in achieving your goals, you have to honestly examine yourself and do matching exercise to see what you have and what you are supposed to have to become an ideal person you wish to be.

Benjamin Franklin, an American inventor, and politician, said that "Your net worth to the world is usually determined by what remains after your bad habits are subtracted from your good ones."

A list of bad habits may include; procrastination, fear of rejection or failure, not assuming responsibility for success or failure, fear of change, being surrounded by negative people, talk about experience instead of accomplishments, request help instead of helping, delve into negative thoughts. Also, may include; snacking non-stop even when not hungry, spending too much time on the couch watching TV, overspending your way into debt, eating too much fast food, behavior that leaves you angry, worried, or stressed all of the time, skipping breakfast, taking too much alcohol, smoking cigarettes.

Napoleon Hill defined procrastination as, "the bad habit of putting off until the day after tomorrow what should have been done the day before yesterday."

An unfortunate thing about this world is that the good habits are much easier to give up than the bad ones. But the only proper way to eliminate bad habits is to replace them with good ones. When you stop bad habits, and you stop long enough, you develop good habits.

It is always hard to knock down bad habits because they happen without our conscious knowledge, they are automatic. As for good habits, when the situation arises for the habit to play and because this is how we have been responding all along, a bad habit will just play. And bad news is, most of the time bad habits are things that we enjoy, so the brain wants to repeat them.

For example, smoking or eating snacks between meals. Scientists say that when we do the habits that give us pleasure they activate a reward center of the brain and so we feel good. Therefore fighting a bad habit needs a plan on how you will go about it. First, identify the habit that you want to fight, and make a deep determination to stop it. The process may include:

Self-discipline and self-awareness - This will alert you when the body wants to engage in a bad habit. Your mind will be vigilant all the time.

Then choose an appropriate approach - Some people decide to stop a bad habit all at once, but some decide to go slow. Like quitting drinking, some just quit at once, like I how I did, but some people choose a gradual approach where they continually reduce the amount of intake let say per week.

Then put obstacles - If you are fighting a bad drinking habit, then you can stop going to pubs. If your problem is too much time on the internet, then disconnect the network until the time you have planned.

Engage in positive behavior - You can decide the time you were using in pubs drinking to be allocated reading books. If your problem is too much time on the internet, then after disconnecting it, just focus on your work. After overcoming the bad habit, you need to reward yourself with something that also will activate your brain but which is positive. This will give you encouragement not to like slip back to the bad habit.

Involve others - By involving close friends, or family members will give you some outside pressure not to give up. Also, they will act as watchers and will remind you when they see any possibility of slipping back.

It is possible, fight bad habit and acquires success habits.

42

WAKE UP EARLY & WORK HARD

Work hard, stay positive, and get up early. It's the best part of the day.
- George Allen, Sr -

After you have acquired a clear vision, you have set up your goals, you have worked on internal qualities like attitude, character, good habits, self-confidence, self-awareness, and emotion intelligence, your body is in good shape and so on and now you are ready to take off, the last gear you have to put in is hard work.

My definition of hard work is working on your goals with a strong dedication, focus, and perseverance for many hours. Many hours includes starting your day early in the morning.

A few years back I joined one business club known as BNI (Business Network International). We used to meet weekly, at 6:30 am. For a business meeting, it seemed very early in the morning. Taking into consideration members had to beat the traffic jam to reach downtown where the meeting used to be held. But the philosophy behind such an early meeting was; start business while your competitors are still asleep.

Most successful people are often the early risers. From Franklin Roosevelt to Barack Obama, from Richard Branson to Charles Darwin, all are known to be early morning people walking towards different personal goals. For 15 years, Starbucks President Michelle Gaas set her alarm for 4:30 a.m. to go running. Mohammed Dewji, Forbes Africa's Person of the Year 2015, wakes up at 4:30am every day to run his business empire. Aliko Dangote, Africa's richest man, wakes up at 5:00am every day. You might be asking yourself, why is rising early such a common trait in successful people? Why do they drag their tired bodies to start the day super early when the rest are still dreaming? Their response should be simple I presume. It is because they know the benefits of doing so.

The winner's mindset - When you get out of your bed and beat that inner voice that tells you not to wake up, you get a sense of control. When your mind wins the battle between staying in bed and waking up, you start your day feeling like a winner already.

When the alarm goes off, and the voice tells you that you went to bed far too late to get up this early, or that five more minutes will not hurt, don't listen! I normally call it a devil's voice, and it gives me one more reason, never to succumb to the devil, and so I wake up.

More time - If you were to get up just one hour early each morning, you would gain 365 working hours in a year. Statistics show that in the US average working hours per day is a bit less than 5 hours. So with an extra 365 working hour per annum, you will have created 73 working days compared to an average person. Wow!! Those are so many days, and a lot can be accomplished in that time.

Avoid distraction - When you wake up early, you are most likely to follow your plan without being distracted by others. It will be easier for you to exercise, or read a book or do your meditation. If you plan to do any of these later in the evening after work, it is always likely to skip because of much interference like, prolonged business meetings or getting unscheduled but important visitors.

Willpower - Time-management expert Laura Vanderkam highlights what makes mornings special and how we can use them more efficiently in her book, *What The Most Successful People Do Before Breakfast,* She says will power is like a muscle, as you work throughout the day its energy gets depleted and at the end of the day you feel tired.

So starting early while your will power is full, with no distractions you will accomplish a lot especially if you focus on the most important activities on your list. There are many more benefits you will enjoy when you master this habit. But if you have tried and still find it difficult, do not give up. You can use a gradual plan;

First Analyze your time use - Some will tell you that they do not wake up early because they go to bed late because of work. You may keep a notebook and every day of a week note how you have used your time. You might be surprised by the outcome. Many find that they waste a lot of hours during the day doing not important activities.

Have a reason - Think of something important you would do by adding one more hour in your day. It could be exercising, or reading a book or beating the traffic and be early in the office. This is because you do not wake up early just for the sake of it but because you have an important reason that will make your life much better.

Make a plan - Once you have made up your mind and you are ready to start, plan your flow of activities. If there are items to be used, prepare them a night before. If you are going to exercise, then have your clothes prepared. If it is reading a book, know which book and keep it ready. If it is beating the traffic, prepare accordingly.

Change gradually - You will likely hit the snooze button and sleep in if you try to switch your habits drastically. So instead of setting your alarm for 5:00 a.m. when you normally get up at 7:00 a.m. set the alarm for 10 minutes earlier each day. To make sure you don't lose sleep, go to bed 10 minutes earlier each night. You may wish to set a bedtime alarm

After mastering the habit of waking up early, you will have created a lot of time that will enable you to accomplish much more than what you used to, and now you will be getting closer to those already successful in your field.

The formula for success: rise early, work hard.

43

SELF-DISCIPLINE

By constant self-discipline and self-control you can develop greatness of character. - **Grenville Kleiser** -

There is an African proverb which says, 'a person who leads you during darkness; you thank him in the morning.' This is how I feel about my secondary school teachers. They were Catholic priests. The life program we followed at that school was like a discipline training camp, not physical, though. I remember we were not allowed to wake up before time, or after time, but strictly on time.

When the bell rings, you get up! We used to have 'silence hours', where no one was allowed to talk to anyone. Sports hours where everyone had to participate. I remember the rules were water tight, and for any misstep, a heavy punishment would be given. As young students, we hated it, but we had no option. We could not understand why such heavy punishments for being 30 seconds late, or for uttering a word during silence hour or for not playing during sports time. But come to think of it now, I cannot thank them enough.

Self-discipline is a very important quality of life that controls your way of life. When you are self-disciplined, means you are in control of your life. I look at it like a steering wheel in a car. Steering wheel will determine where a car goes, whether the car move on its lane or goes into the ditch, the steering wheel will play a great role.

A self-disciplined person controls his thoughts, words, and actions and aligns them with his goal.

Self-mastery is captured well in this quote attributed to various writer:

"Watch your thoughts; they become words;
watch your words; they become actions;
watch your actions; they become habits;
watch your habits; they become character;
watch your character, for it becomes your destiny."

As a person, you may have all the required qualities for success, but if self-discipline is not mastered, success is not guaranteed. Poor self-discipline can let you down anytime, even just before arriving at your destination that is when you are just about to accomplishing your goal.

Self-discipline is about finishing the work you embarked on despite difficulties you encounter along the way, without losing focus, or being destructed by any 'shiny objects' along the way. It is the ability to reject instant gratification and pleasure, for some greater gain, which requires spending effort and time to get it. Zig Ziglar says, it was character that got us out of bed, commitment that moved us into action, and discipline that enabled us to follow through.

I remember a childhood story where self-discipline is well-portrayed about the rabbit and the turtle, who conducted a race. The rabbit was very fast, so he allowed himself to take a nap in the middle of the contest. At the same time, the turtle plodded along, but with willpower and self-discipline he did not despair, kept moving and eventually managed to arrive first at the finish line. Like the turtle, with self-discipline you finish what you start.

I have come to see self-discipline as an invisible magic power. You cannot see, taste, or smell it, but its results are enormous. It can transform one from overweight into lean, from ignorant into expert, from poor into rich, from sadness into happiness. It is the submerged part of the iceberg others do not see when they see your 'genius.' Self-discipline is about willpower, hard work, and persistence.

Good news is that through practicing certain techniques you can also develop your self-discipline. Some of these techniques will be explained below;

Don't wait to 'feel like it' - Self-discipline is about doing what you should do, at the time it should be done even when you do not feel like doing it. When you want to lose weight, and you are required to go to the gym, and you feel like not going, only discipline will push you to go.

Have a self-talk - There is a constant voice in your head, which talks to you all the time. First, try to become an observer of your thoughts. Think about what you are thinking. Are you happy with what your mind is busy about? If not, change the subject. Self-mastery and self-discipline are exactly about that, controlling your thoughts. Tell your mind things it should be thinking about, like good memories of the past events, positive thoughts, motivation, self-encouragement, and self-confidence.

Have a self-audit session - It is important to have a full and honest audit of your character and qualities. You will have, to be honest with yourself to recognize your weaknesses and strengths and align them to your smart goals. Without goals, then self-discipline has no meaning. It is like starting a journey which has no destination and so you will not know what gear will help you along the way. Put plans to turn your weakness into strengths and move your current strengths from good to great.

Avoid shiny objects - Self-discipline is about keeping yourself focused on the goal. Remember that along the way you might get distracted by ideas of shortcuts and quick riches but do not follow them. In life, there is no shortcut to real success. Keep working on your goal.

My take is that self-discipline is what is standing between you and your dreams. Your success is possible only if you are willing to start today, even with baby steps…just start!

44

GET A SUCCESS COACH

A life coach does for the rest of your life what a personal trainer does for your health and fitness. - **Elaine MacDonald** -

A few years ago when I first heard about the concept of having a coach in the corporate world, I could not understand it at all. I was used to having seminars, and training sessions. I thought coaches are for sports only. The concept of having a coach is still new to many executives and business owners in some parts of the world.

There are a variety of coaches for all areas of your life. There are life coaches, organizational coaches, business coaches, sports coaches, executive coaches, career coaches; you name it, and you can probably find a coach to suit your needs. The greatest commonality with all of these types of coaches is that their goal is to help you reach the highest potential in your area of focus.

The richest man on planet, Bill Gates says, everyone needs a coach, no matter who you are, or what you do, as long as you want to improve in what you do, you need a coach. Even those at the top of their game, need a coach to remain there. One of the secrets of highly successful people is that most of them use, in some form or another, a coach to help them get to where they want to be in life or business or both. A coach can help you identify goals and can motivate you to make those goals a reality for your future. Coaching is a powerful relationship in which a client and a coach work to improve the quality of the client's life. Through dialogue, inquiry, goal setting, accountability, and general motivational techniques, the coach supports the client to assume full responsibility for creating a fulfilling life.

Besides the confusion around coaching as a sports metaphor, coaching is often confused with mentoring, counseling and consulting. There are differences;

Mentoring is a relationship where an experienced person shares his or her experience, skills and the know-how's of the particular field with the person being mentored.

Counseling focuses on an individual's psychological well-being, and it focuses on analyzing the past, whereas coaches concentrate on personal and organizational success, how well the person is functioning within the organization and is future focused.

In *consulting*, the consultant gives an opinion to the client on a particular technical issue.

Even if you went to the best schools available or are working for the best companies in the market, or having the best position in your organization or even if you are the star performer in your organization or industry, you need a coach to keep you moving towards excellence. If big multinational companies and many other Fortune 500 have integrated executive coaching into their human resources offerings for company executives why not you and your organization?

The benefits are numerous:

A confidante - A coach is a professional confidante with your best interest in mind. A coach is experienced and will listen to you without being judgmental. He is like a sound board, and you will have a unique opportunity to open up to a person whose best interest is your success.

A coach will help you know and attain your personal or professional goals. Your boss can help you improve, but he will assess you according to organizational goals only. A session with a coach will be about you and how to accomplish your goals only.

Your potential - A coach sees and believes in your potential. A coach will motivate you create your vision and see the future you. You will have to tell the coach your weaknesses and limitations to attain your ideal status. Some people come to find out that their weakness being lack of self-discipline or fear of failure or even low emotional intelligence. The coach will ask tough questions to understand the source of the problem so as to advise strategies to overcome a particular weakness. A goal created by you with guidance of the coach will always be attained.

Expand your thinking - A coach will be asking many questions, and some will be tough to know you better. Many times executives fail to grow because of shallow thinking and limitations they put on themselves because of a lack of self-confidence. Sometimes it is about lack of clear vision or life goals. When there are no challenging goals, the executive may feel he has already arrived at his best potential.

Positivity - Your life will have a lot of twists and turns that are out of your control. A coach will help you to go around, go through or go over obstacles that limit your success. He will help you focus your thoughts on the positive side of the situation and even take advantage of it. He will guide you master self-discipline and increase your self-awareness.

Accountability - A coach will hold you accountable for the achievement of your goals. He will provide you with a sufficient amount of support to help you have the tools, resources and way of thinking to achieve your goals. So executives do not like coaches because they have a, 'I do not want to be told what to do' mentality.

In coaching, accountability may be in the form of 'homework' assignments and motivation, inspiration and encouragement. The coach will always ask for a progress feedback, and if it is negative, he will help you avoid excuses and take full accountability for his success. A coach is a non-judgmental supporter and a key player of your team achievement of your personal and professional success. I have a coach because I want to become a better leadership expert, you need one too if you want success in your life. Everyone needs a coach.

45

PERSONAL BRANDING

The keys to brand success are self-definition, transparency, authenticity and accountability. - **Simon Mainwaring** -

So what is a personal brand? A personal brand is the total experience of someone having a relationship with who you are and what you represent as an individual. It is about deciding to take an active role in the direction of your life. When we talk about personal branding you cannot miss names like Richard Branson, Donald Trump, Oprah Winfrey, Madonna to mention but a few.

Personal branding is the practice of people marketing themselves and their careers as brands. While previous self-help management techniques were about self-improvement, the personal branding concept suggests instead that success comes from self-packaging. It is essentially an ongoing process of establishing a prescribed image or impression in the mind of others about an individual, group or organization.

The keys to brand success are self-definition, transparency, authenticity and accountability. The value of personal brand will be built on the quality of services you can consistently deliver to your clients or target groups. Promotion of your brand will mainly be done through your success stories and achievements recorded in your services, and social media can only supplement it.

The personal branding process is about focusing in on what you are passionate about, carving out a niche for yourself, and consistently adding value to others. It is not about you fighting the competition but about you being excellent at what you do and exceeding customer's expectations. Personal branding is no longer an option but necessary powerful success enabler.

Personal branding enables you to stay unique in your market. Brands are about being noticeable from the cloud. They are unique in the minds of target groups. As a career person or self-employed person, your brand will distinguish you from the rest. If a bank wants to recruit a senior financial controller, they will focus on accountants with banking experience, good interpersonal communication skills, diligent and trustworthy. If you have these qualities, you will be spotted easily.

A personal brand creates awareness for your services. The experience that your client gets is what will make him differentiate you from the rest. In the current world, people buy what they want not what they need. You have to create a desired factor in your services. Someone may like fried chicken, and there are many restaurants that can offer that, but they will go to KFC. Why? Because KFC does it uniquely better. Always look to add value.

Personal branding provides a roadmap to success. After identifying your field and a particular niche lay down a plan to brand yourself to match the expectation of your niche market success will be around the corner. All along the journey, your plan will be your guide. That will result into matching your actions and your communication and so build consistency and authenticity. It will be living your brand.

A personal brand can create a buzz for you. How about having an excellent reputation that precedes you? What if you were told you would be meeting Richard Branson tomorrow, or Donald Trump, or Aliko Dangote, you will be excited. These big names have branded themselves in a way that their brands attract business for them. You too have the opportunity to generate business effortlessly by ensuring your personal brand is positive and regularly being heard, read and discussed mainly by your target niche.

Above all personal branding will portray you as an expert in your field. If you want to gain market recognition, make sure you offer services that will satisfy customers and are also different to what the customer has seen before. This will make you unique, and the client will always want your services. Over time you will develop credibility, respect, and admiration.

Building a brand takes time and constant dedication. Once you lay the groundwork, you will be in a position to eventually reap the benefits.

As you continue to develop your personal brand, stay consistent with your efforts, pay close attention to how your audience responds to your content, and perfect your service until your focus is razor sharp. As an entrepreneur, one of the biggest challenges you will face will be building your brand. The ultimate goal is to set your company and your brand apart from the crowd.

If you develop a strategy without doing appropriate research to back it up, your brand will barely float - and at the speed, industries move at today, brands equally sink fast. Brand yourself and stand out!!

46

FINANCIAL DISCIPLINE

Beware of little expenses. A small leak will sink a great ship.
- Benjamin Franklin -

Many times I have heard stories of people who win lotteries, millions of dollars, but after few years the same people are back to where they used to be, or even worse. This goes down to financial discipline. Financial discipline refers to how well you can contain your spending and saving to the plans that you have set to achieve your monetary goals.

To be successful in life, financial discipline is vital. You can make money in your business, but if management of funds is not good enough, soon you may find yourself in financial distress. Lack of financial discipline cultivates a cycle of living paycheck to paycheck and payment to payment that never ends unless you develop the discipline to escape that life and be different.

Like all other assets, management of funds needs a plan. It does not have to be a complex one but a plan showing what you expect to earn during a particular period, and how you would like to spend it.

The greatest mistake most people do is planning to save some money out of the funds that will remain after expenditures. Big mistake! Always set aside a certain percentage of funds for saving then the rest is allocated for other necessary expenses. You will need to be self-disciplined to utilize your funds according to your set plan. It will be hard to manage funds if you do not have good financial goals to be accomplished. Set your goals, short term, and long term. We all want to take care of our uncertain future. Financial discipline will be essential for you to attain financial freedom at some point in future.

Emergencies are bound to occur in life. The budget has to include an emergency fund which will be used for those truly emergency situations. The way to avoid disaster is to plan for it. You have to have prescribed criteria for what situation you will allow as emergency. In your plan setting aside some funds for your old age, a retirement plan will be a wise idea. With the cost of leaving going up daily, even retired people still have to find jobs. You do not want to be in such a situation, but that can be avoided by starting contributing in a retirement scheme.

Another important item to consider in your budget is contribution for health insurance. Most employers offer this benefit for their employees these days, but if you are self employed, you will have to visit NHIF and the like. You have to make sure that you are well insured as well as your dependants. In some countries, cash health services could be very costly.

After taking into consideration of all current expenditures, also think of investing in some assets like stocks or real estate or any other investment area that is low risk and requires minimum supervision. It is not good to open another business that will consume your time and make you lose focus on your niche market unless your current business is very well established. You have to be very careful with your lifestyle. It happens very often to some people that once success comes and the income increases; they change their lifestyle so much that they find themselves always having to play catch up with their bills.

You make yourself accountable for your spending. This can be done by making sure you track your spending. This will help you stay responsible for your money management. In that regard, put a procedure which will get you think twice before actual spending.

If you are not good at managing your finances, you should consider the help of accountants you know or consultants who can give detailed help. But whatever it is budgeting is vital and so do not wait until funds are already in your bank account to prepare the budget. It will not work!

47

UTILIZE TECHNOLOGY

The new electronic independence re-creates the world in the image of a global village. **- Marshall McLuhan -**

It is not the big that eat the small; it is the fast that eat the slow - **Jason Jennings.** Technology has become a vital part of our existence. However, in recent year technology has taken center stage in almost every aspect of our lives. Even if you are not comfortable with it, you will have to keep up because there is no way one can run away from it.

Technology has revolutionized the way business is done and has made well-established companies close shop because it overtook them. Technology has also made possible for new businesses to play at the same level with the giants and sometimes knock them out. I once heard that when Amazon opened business of selling books online, some big household bookshops went out of business.

Technology has made business global just by a click of a button. Now people can place a product in the market while in New York, and the first buyer can be from Tokyo. The world has indeed become a village. It is no longer impossible to purchase a book from the USA while in Dar es Salaam. It is also possible now to sell a car while in Japan and receive the funds without ever knowing the actual person who bought it. Technology has made the world faceless and flat at the same time.

As an entrepreneur, technology has to be your best friend. You have to find ways to get to know what technology can do to make your life better. Harnessing the power of technology and your urge for excellence in serving your customers can do wonders in how you deliver services and give you an edge above the rest in your field.

Proper use of technology can make you achieve in a short time, what others have achieved after decades of hard work.

Steve Ballmer once said, "the number one benefit of information technology is that it empowers people to do what they want to do. It lets people be creative. It lets people be productive. It lets people learn things they didn't think they could learn before, and so in a sense, it is all about potential." Some think technology is very expensive to purchase, yes it could be expensive but not as expensive as you closing shop and filling for bankruptcy. On the other hand, technology could help you save a lot on labor costs, increase efficiency in service delivery and enhance the quality of products and services.

Marketing for your products can be made very easy by utilizing the power of technology. Your products can be seen by many more people worldwide, and so your market will be the world over.

Sometimes technology can also pose challenges that can also be huge and global. But that should not terrify you and scare you, not at all. In business taking calculated risks is the order of the day. Be bold and step out of your comfort zone. Bill Gates also said that the first rule of any technology used in business is that automation applied to an efficient operation will magnify the efficiency. The second is that automation applied to an inefficient operation will magnify the inefficiency. When I look at the way banks work today, I do not understand how they worked without the current technology.

The amount of transactions per day, the number of people accessing banking services and the capacity to connect information from different parts of the world in microseconds, it just leaves me flabbergasted.

Technology enables executives to access information from their offices and work even when they are in other countries. Gone are those days when an executive would find excuses for being out of the office. The internet and social media are the new tools that can make a lot of difference in business today.

Professionals and businesses, now more than ever, are engaging the social media to facilitate their communication with their prospective customers. Social media is now very powerful. Sites like LinkedIn, Facebook, YouTube and Google can deliver information quicker and deeper than any traditional media like TV and newspapers.

Let the world know who you are because that is the only way the world can understand you and open opportunities for you. Good news is that social media is mostly free and opportunities are worldwide. My take is, use technology as much as possible.

Talk to experts and seek their advice on how better to harness the power of technology and the creativity of your staff in making the company perform better and access new customers and new markets.

48

WORK-FAMILY BALANCE

*A person has got to balance work and life and family in order
to be a balanced person.* **- P. J. O'Rourke -**

'Work well, live well.' This used to be one of our mottos when I was working with one of my former employers. I remember my CEO used to joke with us saying, be careful because soon your child will call you uncle. This is when he would find us working late. My employer encouraged people to balance their work time and family time.

However, we kept working late almost every day, sometimes till midnight, because in a multinational organization there are many reporting lines and deadlines are very tight, especially when a company is listed on the New York Stock Exchange and London Stock Exchange. It was a tough experience that made me have very little time with my family.

'Work-life balance' is the philosophy that has been advocated by many sociologists with excellent logics behind it, but I see it falls under the category of 'easier said than done.' From what I have been hearing from the people I meet, for some employers, a mention of work-life balance in their recruitment interview will automatically disqualify you because they are totally allergic to such philosophies. There is an African proverb that says, 'let the donkey die, but the cargo has to be delivered.' That is the philosophy of such employers, who see those leaving office a few minutes after official working hours as lazy, not committed to their work and not loyal.

Many people encounter situations like these, and you might be one of them. Work remains important for your survival while family is very important for your life. You have to make a choice of where you stand and how you stand.

The truth is, you need your job very much. You need growth in your career; you need to meet your planned goals, and you need to make more money to make your family live a better life. In that regard, you have to meet the expectations of your employer. You have to work hard and work smart to earn your promotion.

Your family needs you, some say, family comes first. They say any time spent with your family is a greatest valued gift that any other material gifts you may buy for them. It is always a good feeling spending time with your spouse and your lovely children. I always feel very happy just being around them, watching Tv together and my most satisfying moment at home is sitting at the dinner table together as a family.

To me, planning is always my fallback position. For anything to move in life, planning comes first. You will have to evaluate your life, and see how important your current job is. Look at your family, assess the important obligations and try to see how you can match them with the time available for you after work.

It is you who will determine where the balance is. Your plan will help you find that balance. You have to make sure that the time you get after work is utilized very well for important obligations. Allocate most of your free time after for your family. Friends are important, plan time for friends and go out Sunday afternoon to watch some soccer matches and exchange some ideas. Ladies the same way, plan some quality time with your friends, I am sure you will have a lot to talk about after not seeing each other for some time. Friends are important but their time has to be also planned.

You will have to find the best use of your weekends when you are not at work. Plan your family shopping outings and have lunch at a hotspot in downtown where you can get a new taste of food other than that what the housemaid cooks for you every day.

I normally spend Sunday evenings at the movie theater with family because I find it as one of the places the whole family can enjoy. When I go out with my wife and children, I feel more satisfaction, and it helps parents bond better with children. During the week everyone is busy, both of us go to work while our, children go to school, so we have no time for each other.

Also, plan for a family vacation once in a year. This can be when children are on leave so that you can all be free. According to your budget, you may go to another city where you will do nothing else but enjoy with your family. If your budget is good enough, then plan for a long safari to the Serengeti to see the world's most beautiful ecosystem or go to Zanzibar to enjoy exotic cuisine and see history with your own eyes.

They say work-life balance is easier said than done, but they do not say it is impossible. So if it is possible, make it so. All successful people work hard and play hard. When you find that balance, your life will be a happy one. You will be free of stress. You will neither carry office problems at home nor will you shift family issues to your workplace. You will have a good working relationship with your boss because deadlines and targets will be met and you will earn promotions as opportunities occur. You will have a good rapport with your colleagues, but no gossip time because you have to complete your to-do list for that day and join your family as early as possible.

49

LEARN TO NEGOTIATE

You do not get what you want. You get what you negotiate.
- Harvey Mackay -

Negotiating is a part of everyday life, but in business, it is extremely vital to your success. Poor negotiation can affect a company just as quickly as losing an important customer. I have noted that many negotiation techniques seem to be common, but it is not abnormal for people to get caught up in the emotion of the moment and ignore their basic instincts. Ego, luck, and emotion have no place in a successful negotiation. It takes an iron gut, homework, street smarts, focus on the big picture and self-discipline. These keys will unlock your ability to get the best deal possible under any circumstances.

As an executive or an entrepreneur, you have to know that negotiations skills are very crucial for your success. As the famous saying goes, *" In life you do not get what you deserve but what you negotiate."* So for any negotiation encounter, you have to do thorough preparation.

While preparing for negotiation, study members of the other side's team, if possible, and get to know their strengths and weaknesses. Find ways to capitalize on the weakness of the counterpart. Get to know why they are in the deal, let's say it is a real estate property, and they are selling, and you want to purchase the property.

Get to know the reason why they are selling. If they are in liquidity problem, and they are under pressure to get the funds to settle their bills, then capitalize on it, or if supply in the market is high then know how to use the information to your advantage. The first offer is very important. So if you are the one negotiating a contract for service to the client, then start with the highest price, but not ridiculously high.

Do not be afraid to ask, because if you do not ask, you will not receive. From there the counterpart will start bargaining on that base trying to lower your price. Always know your rock bottom price and you may give in slowly from the first offer.

Give a clear impression to the counterpart that you are knowledgeable on the subject you are talking about. This will act as a defense from the counterpart who may decide to call a bluff and confuse you with some statistics.

Listening is an important skill at the negotiation table. Do not utter a word without thinking twice, because you will not have any opportunity to retrieve your statement otherwise you lose credibility.

Leave your ego at the entrance door to the negotiation room. Remember this is business not personal, so do not tag your arguments on people. Stick to facts and logic. Find common ground and show your counterpart the benefit of the offer you are giving and how they will also benefit. Study the words and body language of your counterpart and try to know whether your points are landing or not. Always keep calm, do not lose your cool during negotiations even if situation gets tense.

Always look at a long term benefit and not quick gratification. Look at the big picture. Try to see benefits of the deal that the counterpart has not recognized. Such as the market boom when you are buying an item or price deterioration in the market.

Leave the table by asking adjournment till another day if you see no notable movement. Never radiate any sign that will indicate you are under pressure to close the deal. Make sure that you do not close the deal on the losing side; rock bottom should be a win-win situation.

When the deal is closed, make sure details of the contract are well documented and clear. Do not just rush to sign since of the money because all other clauses in the contract are very important. These should include offer price (in proper denomination), statement of work (scope), identification and quantities of goods or services, delivery schedule, performance incentives (if any), express warranties (if any), terms and conditions, and any documents incorporated by reference.

Do not agree on the general statement on contracts like, 'this is a standard contract', or 'others also have signed the same.' Always make sure you read all clauses in the contract and you are in total agreement with each of them. If there is any clause that you do not agree with, do not sign and ask for explanation or clarification.

My take is that negotiation skills are very important for your success. Mastery of this skill will help you avoid future financial loss and reputation damage. As a rule never, negotiate or sign a contract while over excited. It is advisable to ask a lawyer or any knowledgeable third party for a second opinion if possible.

50

SUPER CUSTOMER SERVICE

A satisfied customer is the best business strategy of all.
- Michael LeBoeuf -

Tears dropped from his eyes; his voice could no longer be heard, he reached for his handkerchief, and he could no longer resist the strength of passion he had about the subject under discussion. After 30 seconds, he raised his head and asked to be excused for what had happened. All people kept quiet; no one knew how to respond to the situation. Here was the CEO expressing his deep passion for excellent customer service.

We had had many management meetings, but this one touched us in a unique way. Our organization was one of the best performing in the market, and we were the fastest growing in the region. The tears from the CEO were tears of passion.

We wanted to keep the pace and even break our record, we wanted to lead from the front and show the world that even at our size, we could be a shining example of excellence, and nothing but excellent customer service could take us where we wanted. In this era, almost all companies can offer good products that meet the needs of the customer. The difference is the human touch; the relationship is what counts. Many customers switch from one service provider to another, just because of poor human touch at the reception counter of the company. Just that!

It is now imperative for companies to find new means to make their services stand out in the industry. Companies have to ensure that the customer gets a very memorable experience when he comes in contact with any staff in the company.

Over the last century growth of companies depended very much on sales teams which went out like an army of ants to try and convince the customers that they need their product. This style is no longer working. This is a customer service era; customer experience is what counts. It has already been proved beyond doubt that there is no powerful method of marketing than a word from a satisfied customer to his or her peers. This word of mouth will help your company spend much less on media advertisements.

Excellent customer service is what will result in repeat sales. If you want your brand to lead in the market, make sure that what you offer in the market is not just the best but make it so excellent that no one will ever beat it even if they wanted to. You will have to raise the bar so high that your competitors will always be playing catch up.

Create a culture of looking for excellence so much so that if you think your product lacks excellence you do not deliver it, even if the customer might not notice easily. The company that is looking for excellence makes sure that all employees live the culture, not just front office staff.

When excellence is what is expected from all employees, then you are not worried because your image will be safe with any staff member. Many companies make mistakes of training some front office staff and forget that at some point even the so-called back office staff will meet customers, people in finance, or human resources department. When a customer walks in the office, he should never be told that is not my job, or it is not our department. For the customer, the staff he meets at the company's office is the company itself.

IBM founder Thomas Watson is attributed with saying, "if you want to achieve excellence, you can get there today. As of this second, quit doing less-than-excellent work". He nailed it on the head, no more to add to that.

Excellent service includes fast services too. I remember there was a small bank that entered the market, and everyone kept asking how they would survive in the market with a cut throat competition. But what was observed in just six months is purely like the story of David versus Goliath. The small bank capitalized on excellent customer service within a short time and set a new record in the industry such that other banks had to learn to catch up. The small bank had seen the weakness in the market and quashed the status quo. This is now a fast world, and all expect it to be like that.

We see drive through fast foods. Fast coffee, express dry cleaning, ATMs and even pizza delivery time is getting shorter. With this pattern, the only way to survive in business is to make it as easy as possible for people to do business with you regardless of the size of your company.

The other way to improve customer service in a company is by empowering employees to solve some customer challenges on their own instead of waiting for a very senior manager. Ritz-Carlton, winner of the 1992 Malcolm Baldridge National Quality Award had given every employee the autonomy to serve customers in any way they deem appropriate, which includes giving hotel housekeepers the ability to spend up to $2,000 to solve a customer problem. That is empowerment at its best!

You must remember that customers spend their hard earned money at your company, and they will expect nothing less than excellence. They expect to have easy access to you, and they expect their issues to be resolved to their satisfaction.

To attain excellence in customer service, the company has to ensure that all staff learn and master critical skills embedded in customer service.

The first one will be for all employees to learn the art of listening. Listening is a core quality of customer service. When a customer walks in or calls the company, the receiving staff should listen and understand what the customer needs. There should be no jumping to conclusion. Make a customer feel that she is valued and respected.

Thorough knowledge of products is crucial to all staff. A customer on the other side should always feel that all employees have the same goals, the same mission, and the same vision. That will make him have confidence with the whole company and not just one person.

Staff should always have a pleasant language, should be calm, confident, smiling and positive minded. They should be able to read the mood of the customer and communicate in a way that would not upset him. As well, when the customer is harsh or impatient, they should be mature enough not to get emotional too. Staff should always be ready to go out of their way to meet customer's expectation and may exceed them.

The importance of excellent customer service for your survival can not be over emphasized. Just do what Steve Jobs said, "Be a yardstick of quality..."

www.ingramcontent.com/pod-product-compliance
Lightning Source LLC
Chambersburg PA
CBHW020332160726
47992CB00004B/1815